COMMUNISTS IN THE DEMOCRATIC PARTY

Author: Concerned Voters, Inc.
(Wilson C. Lucom, Chairman)

Published by:
Concerned Voters Inc.
P.O. Box 40309
Washington, D.C. 20016 NW

TABLE OF CONTENTS

GLOSSARY

ACFPC	Arms Control & Foreign Policy Caucus
CBC	Congressional Black Caucus
CISPES	Committee in Solidarity with the People of El Salvador
CNFMP	Coalition for a New Foreign & Military Policy
CNSS	Center for National Security Studies
CPLAN	Communist Party Legislative Action Network
CPSU	Communist Party of the Soviet Union
CPUSA	Communist Party of the U.S.A.
DNC	Democratic National Committee
IADL	International Association of Democratic Lawyers
IPS	Institute for Policy Studies
NLG	National Lawyers Guild
SANE	Committee for a Sane Nuclear Policy
SDS	Students for a Democratic Society
USPC	U.S. Peace Council
WPC	World Peace Council
WSP	Women Strike for Peace

Communist Code Words

"All People's Front" or **"All People's Unity"**
Coalitions of organizations being manipulated to cooperate to promote Communist goals.

"Independent Forces"
Special interest groups now operating within the Democratic Party, which the Communists expect eventually to split off and become "independent", i.e., pro-communists

"Progressive"
Used by Communists to denote people or organizations that are pro-communist, or promoting a Communist line. (Many people calling themselves "progressives" are not Communists but may unwittingly aid the Communists.)

Chapter 1

Introduction

The purpose of this book is to alert the American voters that the Communists, in their publications, say they have joined and infiltrated the Democratic Party. When you finish reading this book, you will agree there are Communists in the Democratic Party. Read how openly and brazenly they say so.

American voters, as a whole, will not vote for an openly-admitted Communist. But any Communist who has not declared himself can easily join and infiltrate the Democratic Party without renouncing Communism. Gus Hall, General Secretary of the Communist Party U.S.A., says that such a person is "riding two horses," one Communist, the other Democrat. This Communist may now call himself a "Left-wing Democrat" or a "Progressive Democrat."

The unknowing Democratic voters will now vote for this Communist because he calls himself a Democrat. Most Democratic voters, out of loyalty, vote the straight Democratic Party ticket. This is how a Democrat votes for a Communist without knowing it. He thinks he is voting for a Democrat but instead is voting for a Communist.

Once in the Democratic Party, the Communist then proceeds to promote Communist policies and objectives and even to get Communist-backed resolutions into the Democratic Party Platform. He or she also votes in Congress in ways that support the national interests of the Soviet Union instead of the national interests of the United States.

Just five or ten Senators and Representatives are enough to influence the entire 540 members of Congress. These five or ten legislators can influence the Senate or House to vote in the national interest of the Soviet Union by voting parallel to the Communist line.

The Communists have said openly in their publications that they can get five to ten Senators and Congressmen to vote their way by using the Communist Party Legislative Action Network, CPLAN, which will be explained later in this book.

How does it happen that five or ten legislators can influence the entire Congress to vote the Communist line when most Senators and Representatives are patriotic Americans? Democratic party loyalty is the unfortunate answer. A Democrat who is also a concealed Communist finally gets on an important committee or even to be the Chairman. Once in this position, he or she can introduce a bill following the Communist line, or influence other Democrats to vote against a bill aiding Democracy or opposing Communism. Out of party loyalty all Democratic members then feel obliged to vote as the concealed Communist chairman recommends. If a member does not vote as recommended, then the chances of ever getting on an important committee are nil. He or she is considered "unreliable."

This Congressional disciplined voting is called "reliability." If you are not reliable to vote the Democratic Party line, you are out of favor for ever getting on important committees, let alone ever becoming chairman. In this way the individual Senator or Representative votes the Communist Party line without ever knowing that he or she is doing so.

This is how Communist policies and objectives also become Democratic policies and objectives. Because the Democrats are in the majority in the Senate and the House of Representatives, these Communist goals are then voted into the Laws of the United States without most Democrats even knowing that they are following or paralleling the Communist line.

What is really functioning in the Democratic party and in your Congress is, on one hand, a coalition of Communists and their non-Communist helpers and, on the other hand, regular Democrats who are not Communist and do not follow the Communist Party line. The Communists in the Democratic Party are concealed so the American voters do not know that this condition exists.

This concealment of Communists in the Democratic Party is much more dangerous than an open coalition between the Democrats and the Communists. Of course the objective is the same – the eventual installation of a Communist government.

Coalitions are dangerous. These coalitions work mainly to the advantage of the Communists. Take Czechoslovakia, for example. In 1948 the Communists took over after just three years of a coalition government. Imagine, in just three years the Communists were in complete control of Czechoslovakia. This is frightening.

Dr. Gerhart Niemeyer's book: *Communists in Coalition Governments,* really exposes how the Communists operate when they form a coalition government. Their objective is always World Revolution with the installation of a Communist government. This Communist purpose never deviates.

In Dr. Niemeyer's book, he says: "The records show that coalition governments in which Communists participate end in one of three ways; in the eventual ouster of the Communists, in armed conflict, or in a Communist takeover of total power. The reason is clear. For the Communists, unlike other partners in a coalition, the alliance is but a technical maneuver within an overall strategic plan. The ultimate goal is not effective national government. It is World Revolution." He lays special emphasis on the concept of the United Front (a temporary alliance of the Communists with all other "working class" parties and "democratic parties of the national bourgeoisie.")

As Professor Niemeyer points out, such alliances indeed are "'fronts' – devices for rallying popular support and providing a cloak of 'respectability' behind which the Communists can consolidate their control of all social and governmental institutions and, ultimately, their monopoly of power." The author suggests that "first counsel of self-protection against Communist totalitarianism is the realization that with the Communists, no common cause or binding agreement is possible, except on their terms."

This last statement is very important because no matter how many "temporary alliances" or coalition governments, the Communist objective remains the same: THE EVENTUAL INSTALLATION OF A COMMUNIST GOVERNMENT.

This book will provide the evidence of this dangerous development in the U.S., not by making unconfirmed accusations, but with quotations from the Communist's own official publications. To have one of America's two major parties increasingly influenced by the agents of a foreign power is a tragic and dangerous development in our history.

This book also will outline recommendations for purging this great party, the heirs of Thomas Jefferson, Andrew Jackson Woodrow Wilson, Franklin D. Roosevelt, Jack Kennedy, Hubert Humphrey, Scoop Jackson and countless others, of such Communist influence before it is too late.

This alarming trend has been almost totally ignored up to now by politicians of both parties for fear of being labelled "McCarthyites." The Communists will charge this book is "McCarthyism." It definitely is not "McCarthyism" as will be shown.

Websters Third New International Dictionary defines "McCarthyism" as follows:

"A political attitude of the mid-twentieth century closely allied to know-nothingism and characterized chiefly by opposition to elements held to be subversive and by the use of tactics involving <u>personal attacks on individuals</u> by means of widely publicized <u>indiscriminate allegations</u> esp. on the basis of <u>unsubstantiated charges</u>." (Emphasis added.)

The Communist charge of "McCarthyism" is disproved and dismissed at the outset. This book does not make personal attacks on individuals by means of indiscriminate allegations on the basis of unsubstantiated charges. It is the <u>Communists</u>, themselves, <u>who publish that they are in the Democratic Party</u>.

Why haven't you read about this situation in *The New York Times*, *The Washington Post*, or other newspapers? A long time ago, probably so long ago that succeeding reporters did not know about it, these newspapers tacitly agreed to rarely, if ever, mention in depth the subject of Communism. To this day they rarely, if ever, mention Communist participation in any organizations in the United States. The newspapers will deny such a practice, but the proof is the lack of mention of Communist participation in marches, demonstrations and other operations.

If Americans knew there were Communists involved in the demonstrations, they would boycott the demonstrations. Not knowing this fact, Americans support a visible cause like Peace as being a good cause, which it is when not infiltrated by Communists. The Communists, on the other hand, only use these causes to promote and advance Communism. Most of the very big demonstrations are either allied with or directed by Communists. The planning and the logistics needed are far beyond the resources of individuals. Such demonstrations need a well-organized group or party behind them.

The defeat in Congress of aid to the Nicaraguan Contras, influenced by the Communist's CPLAN and Communist-allied demonstrations, was a shocking betrayal of the national interest of the United States by the majority of Democratic Congressmen. It is in the national interest of the United states to have all countries of the world Democratic. It is in the national interest of the Soviet Union to have all countries Communist.

The Congressional Record of February 3, 1988, shows that the following leading Democratic Congressmen voted against aid to the Nicaraguan Freedom Fighters, who were fighting for Democracy against the Communist government of Nicaragua:

Les Aspin	Charles Hayes
Les AuCoin	Robert Kastenmeier
Ed Boland	Joseph Kennedy
David Bonior	Peter Kostmayer
Don Bonker	Jim Leach
Barbara Boxer	Ed Markey
George Brown	Nancy Palosi
John Conyers	J. J. Pickle
George Crockett	Charles Rangel
Ron Dellums	Peter Rodino
Tom Downey	Dan Rostenkowski
Mervyn Dymally	Gus Savage
Don Edwards	Pat Schroeder
Mike Espy	Steve Solarz
Barney Frank	Gerry Studds
Sam Gejdenson	Morris Udall
Richard Gephardt	Ted Weiss
William Gray	Howard Wolpe
Lee Hamilton	Sidney Yates

This list includes only the most prominent names. Additional members voted in the same "unknown helping of Communism" way, enough to defeat aid to the Contras by the slim margin of 219 to 211 votes in the House of Representatives. All these Congressmen unknowingly helped Communism by voting against aid to the anti-communists in Nicaragua.

Fortunately, the Nicaraguan Freedom Fighters were able to survive long enough to keep pressure on the Sandinista Government. This, combined with additional moral pressure from the other Central American states and the international community, caused the Sandinista government to allow the elections of February 25, 1990. In spite of massive Sandinista harassment of the opposition, this election resulted in the defeat of the Sandinista Communist government.

Because the newspapers and other polls, including the *Washington Post*, showed Communist President Ortega leading by 20% to 80% of the voters, Ortega scheduled free elections believing he was going to win. He never thought he would be defeated. If he had, he would never have scheduled the elections. When the results came in, he was the most shocked man in Nicaragua.

Many leading Democrats still continue to parallel the Communist line, being against aid to the democratically-elected government of El Salvador. For example, as late as February 6, 1990, Senators Edward Kennedy and John Kerry introduced a bill to cut off all aid to El Salvador just a few days after El Salvador's President Cristiani had come to Washington to discuss the need for such support. This bill was backed by four other Democratic Senators: Barbara Mikulski of Maryland, Paul Simon of Illinois, Alan Cranston of California and Brock Adams of Washington state.

The Senators and Congressmen who vote against providing aid to the government of El Salvador are doing nothing less than opposing the democratically-elected government in that area and paralleling the Communist line. Whether they wittingly follow the Communist line or unwittingly parallel the Communist line, they are helping the Communist cause and the national interest of the Soviet Union.

Make no mistake about it – "No Aid to El Salvador" is the <u>official Communist line</u>. The proof of this is found in the Communist official magazine, *Political Affairs*, February 1989, Vol. 2, LXVILL, page 12 as follows:

> **"End all aid to the Contras in Central America and Afghanistan."**

This Communist line was repeated in the official Communist newspaper the *People's Daily World* of January 30, 1990 when it published:

> **"Last weekend's meeting of the Communist Party, USA resolved to: 3. Mobilize to build the March 24 demonstration in Washington, D.C. demanding an <u>end to military aid to El Salvador</u> and intervention in Central America."**

You will observe the Communists are mobilizing and building this demonstration. Yet, your Democratic Congressmen vote paralleling this official Communist line and are against providing adequate aid to El Salvador. Why is this so? Because there are hidden Communists riding "two horses" joined by their non-communist helpers in the Democratic Party.

We are supplying aid to the democratically-elected government of El Salvador because it is in our national interest that El Salvador be Democratic, not Communist. The Salvadoran Communist guerrillas are fighting to overthrow this democratic Salvadoran government. If we limit or cut off aid to the Salvadoran government, then the Communist guerrillas could win because they are continuing to receive supplies from the Soviet Union or its satellites. This would result in a Communist government, which is in the national interest of the Soviet Union.

Some Senators and Congressmen have said the El Salvadoran government should negotiate with the Communist rebels. Negotiate what? The El Salvadoran Communists pretended to boycott the elections and tried to intimidate non-communists from voting. This intimidation failed and those in favor of a Democratic government won. Those favoring the Communists lost.

Though they lost in the general election, the Communist guerrillas still fight on, hoping to overthrow the Democratic government and install a Communist government. So what is there to negotiate about? The size of the El Salvadoran Army? The Communists say it is too large. It must remain at its present size as long as the Communists mount military offensives against the government. If the Communist rebels stop fighting, then and only then can President Cristiani reduce the size of the army. Until that time comes, he must keep the army at its present size. It is the Communist rebels who are really keeping the army large.

The Communist strategy is that the FMLN, a Communist military revolutionary military force, is fighting to overthrow the Democratic El Salvadoran government so El Salvador can become a Communist state. This is against our national interest.

We must mention the charge of Army brutality that was raised because someone, possibly a very small section of the Army, killed six Jesuit priests in San Salvador. Democratic Senators and Congressmen are constantly bringing this up as their reason to oppose aid to the El Salvadoran government.

Some of the Catholic Jesuit order have bought the Communist line of "Liberation Theology." Liberation Theology calls for the Catholic priests to work with the Communists in the common cause of helping the poor, even though the Communists are the "anti-Christs." Communism officially declares its government is atheistic, against all religions, including Catholicism.   It is inexplicable and disturbing that the Jesuits would work with their enemy.

This is wrong because the Jesuit priests can help the poor without allying themselves with the Communist guerrillas in the name of helping the poor. Because the Communists use "temporary alliances" with any group, including priests, their sole objective is to help advance Communism – not the cause of helping the poor. This is only a tactic.

The following on the six priests is the personal opinion of this author. Soldiers just do not go about indiscriminately killing people. There has to be a cause for them to do so. What is the cause? When the priests supply arms or act as conduits for arms to the rebels, the priests are no longer just priests, but are also "soldiers" fighting on the side of the enemy.   Unfortunately, the priests are helping the Communist rebels. When they do so, they surrender their protection solely as priests.

This is not peacetime in El Salvador, but a time of armed war between the government and the Communist rebels. Both sides are killing each other and the people who aid and supply them. A thorough investigation will show the priests were not just priests but were helping the Communist rebels.

The Communist guerrillas have killed many Salvadoran civilians who were aiding the government

army. Yet seldom, if ever, do you read of the rebels
killing civilians in El Salvador. Many thousands –
much more than six priests – were killed by the
Communist rebels. The Democratic senators and
Congressmen should look at the overall picture of
how many civilians the Communist rebels are killing,
instead of focusing on six priests. When mentioning
the six Jesuit priests killed, why are the Democratic
Congressmen silent on the assassinations of 20 local
Mayors by the Salvadoran Communist rebels? This
far outweighs the deaths of six priests.

Why have these Democratic Congressmen remained silent about the *New York Times* May 27,
1990 article:

EL SALVADOR REBELS FAULTED
FOR EXECUTIONS

"SAN SALVADOR, May 26, 1990,
(Reuters) Leftist Salvadoran rebels have
carried out several hundred executions
since the early 1980's after trials in
revolutionary courts, the Americas Watch
human-rights group said today.

"In some cases, the left guerrilla
organization Farbundo Marti National
Liberation Front had assassinated
opponents without a trial. Americas
Watch said it rejected rebels assertions
that revolutionary courts operating in
guerrilla-held areas met international
standards of law.

"The rebels do not require any
member of their ad hoc court to have any
legal training or competence, the group
said in a report. 'That the authority to

impose the death penalty is vested in individuals apparently unskilled in the law
is appallingly indecent.' The report said
the practice 'utterly deprives the
accused of a basic guarantee necessary
for his or her defense.'"

The Communist rebels also assassinated
Salvadoran Attorney General Roberto Garcia Alvarez,
former Supreme Court President Francisco Jose
Guerro and rightist leader, Francisco Peccorini
Letona.

This shows the bias of your Democratic congressmen against the democratically-elected government of El Salvador – a bias that favors the
Communist rebels. Six Jesuit priests are killed and
the Democratic Congressmen endlessly keep repeating this fact. Several hundreds of executions including the Attorney General of El Salvador and the
former Supreme Court President are carried out by
the Communist rebels, the Communist FMLN, yet
these Democratic Congressmen completely ignore
these horrible killings, executions and assassinations
and just dwell on the six priests. Because of these
six priests, the Democratic Congressmen are against
aid to El Salvador, which is also parallel to the
Communist line.

Jennifer Casolo, an American in El Salvador,
was found to have a large cache of arms buried in her
backyard. Her compound was walled and it was
impossible for arms not to have not gone in by her
front door. Yet, she was set free because of pressure
from the United States. Her claim of not knowing
those arms were in her backyard is dubious. Her di-
ary, which was also found buried beside the cache,
revealed she sympathized with the rebels. She said
she did not know anything about the arms. We leave
it to the reader to decide.

The American Communists and their helpers launched Jennifer Casolo on a nationwide speaking tour. This was part of the Communist propaganda operation. She kept repeating the "big lie" and even many Senators and Congressmen eventually believed her ridiculous story. Hitler said in *Mein Kampf* that if a "big lie" is repeated enough times, it becomes the truth – even though it is untrue.

The same Democrats who paralleled the Communist Party line of "no aid to the Contras" are once again paralleling the Communist Party line of "no aid to El Salvador." Their votes are against the national interest of the United States and unknowingly in the national interest of the Soviet Union.

Let the concealed Communists and their non-communist helpers go to the Communist Party where they belong. They do not belong in the Democratic Party because they are anti-democratic.

This book is a determined effort to bring the Communist issue out into the open and finally get some action. As the author, I am a long-time Democrat and am concerned about this condition in my own party. My father was also a Democrat. I was named after that great Democratic president, Woodrow Wilson, who led this country against another tyranny, the Kaiser's Germany.

For many years this country has been facing an even more dangerous adversary, the world-wide Communist movement Our Democratic party has grown steadily weaker in meeting this threat, more infiltrated and manipulated by the agents or sympathizers of this Communist adversary. That is what this book deals with.

The exciting developments in Eastern Europe have led many to believe that Communism is no longer a menace. It is true that the Soviet Union is facing huge economic and nationalities problems. Its satellites in Eastern Europe appear to be throwing out the old Communist bosses and bringing in newer more liberal regimes. But there is evidence that the Communists are still a threat to the United States and the free world. These can be summarized briefly as follows:

1 – In Asia, the Communist regimes in Viet Nam, Laos, North Korea, and China remain in power, as totalitarian and brutal as ever.

2 – In almost all Eastern European countries that appear to be ousting the former Communist regimes, the Communist parties in fact still run the Intelligence Services and, in most cases, the military. This ominous fact was summarized in a major article in the *New York Times* as of December 31, 1989 (p.15). These facts coincide with the recent statement by William Webster, Director of the CIA, that "Soviet intelligence activities directed against the U.S. have not abated. In fact they have increased."

3 – Since Gorbachev took office, arms production has continued to exceed the U.S. volumes by large margins, in spite of his claims of cutting back military spending. Since 1981 Soviet production has exceeded U.S. production by the following ratios:

Intercontinental Ballistic Missiles	4-1
Tanks	3-1
Artillery	8-1
Bombers	4-1.

Why are they building up land-based artillery eight to one? This is not defensive but offensive. In anti-missile devices the Soviets are still turning out a large volume of quality products while we produce none. They continue to turn out one nuclear submarine every seven weeks. Such submarines are offensive units only, designed to strike the U.S. with ballistic missiles.

4 – In the last three years, the Soviets have been building up their forces around Murmansk and other northern regions close to the Norwegian and Swedish borders. These forces now include 446 naval aircraft, 140 submarines, a Naval Spetsnaz brigade, 2 motorized rifle divisions, 22 major air bases and 18 secondary airfields, 9 submarine bases, 70 strategic air defense SAM systems, etc. All of these forces have almost no defense value and are only designed for offense, i.e., invading Norway and Sweden to outflank NATO and to interdict the Atlantic sea lanes to cut off U.S. support for NATO if the Soviets launch an invasion of Western Europe.(1)

5 – Soviet Aid to Cuba is not being stopped. It is to be continued for another five years, which is an additionally long time. Why do the Soviets continue to send aid, support, money and Soviet MIG fighters to Cuba? Because, they have not changed their ultimate objective of controlling the world - sooner or later.

Cuba is supplying arms to the Communist rebels in Latin America and the Soviet Union through Cuba is continuing to supply these Communist rebels because they advance the cause of Communism in Central and South America.

The Soviet policy of world conquest has not changed; otherwise, they would immediately, not five years from now, stop sending financial support to Cuba's Castro, particularly because Castro has split with Gorbachev and does not support Glasnost or

Perestroika.   Yet the Soviet Union continues to support Cuba financially. This action speaks for itself - continued efforts for world domination by Communism.

6 – The Soviets also continue to ship massive amounts of arms to the Communist regime in Angola, which has launched a new offensive against the anti-Communist UNITA forces. And Soviet aid to the Communist government in Afghanistan continues at the rate of more that $250 million <u>per month</u>, while we have almost stopped aid to the anti-Communist Mujihadeen.

If Gorbachev is sincere about disarmament and Glasnost and concerned about his disastrous civilian economy, why is he still pushing these huge purely <u>offensive</u> programs in arms production in the Murmansk region and the Third World? We cannot assume that the Soviet's expansionist ambitions have ceased until they stop sending arms to El Salvador, Angola, Afghanistan, and elsewhere. Until they stop sending weapons, they cannot be trusted as wanting peace. We should look at what the Soviets are <u>doing</u>, not what Gorbachev is <u>saying</u>.

So although the developments in Eastern Europe are heartening, we cannot assume the threat of Communism or Soviet expansionism has stopped. It is a major objective of the Communists under the leadership of the Soviet Union that all nations of the world eventually become Communist, that is, to have a Marxist-Leninist government in every country. In contrast, it is in the national interest of the United States that all countries be democratic – to have a multi-party system, a free press, freedom to own private property, freedom of religion, free labor unions, a free market economy, and all the other freedoms.

Every American has the right to ask his or her Senators and Representatives in Congress:

"Are you for Democracy or are you for Communism? If you are for Democracy in Latin America, which is in the national interest of the United States, then you must oppose having Communists controlling each Central American government.

"You cannot just be neutral, which benefits the Communist cause. Being neutral means the U.S. does nothing militarily to help a democratic country while the Communists are shipping large quantities of arms and supplies to the Communist rebels. If this continues, the Communist rebels will eventually win. Another country will will have fallen to Communism while our United States Congress does nothing to help."

Why, at times, does the U.S. Congress do nothing? This book tells why – because there are hidden Communists or Communist helpers in Congress who vote for the national interest of the Soviet Union instead of the United States' national interest.

Remember that a person does not have to be a card-carrying member of the Communist Party to help Communism. In fact, non-communists who help Communism are more valuable to the Communist Party than its members. As Senator Hubert Humphrey said in 1966, "It is unimportant whether a man is a Communist. What is important is <u>does he help Communism</u>."

Eudocio Ravines, a former Communist, testified before the Senate Subcommittee on Internal Security in 1955. He said:

> "We must always remember that one sympathizer is generally worth more than a dozen militant Communists. A university professor, who without being a party member, lends himself to the interests of the Soviet Union, is worth more than a hundred men with party cards. . . The writer, who without being a party member, defends the Soviet Union, the union leader who is outside our ranks but defends Soviet international policy <u>is worth more than a thousand party members</u>."(2) (Emphasis added.)

It is plain that members of Congress who are unknowingly manipulated into supporting the national interests of the Soviet Union instead of the United States are worth their weight in gold to the Communist Party. This is a shocking state of affairs. It shows how "the hidden Communists" and their helpers in the Democratic Party have been able to help Communism and hurt Democracy.

Many examples will be given later in this book. First, the next chapter will provide some quotations from Communist leaders themselves on their policy of infiltration and manipulation of the Democratic Party's Liberal and Progressive wings.

NOTES

1. *Air Forces Journal,* 12/89, p. 70.
2. Senate Internal Security Subcommittee Hearings, 1955, p. 83.

Chapter 2

The Evidence – Communist Statements

Communist objectives to infiltrate and manipulate the Democratic Party can be illustrated by direct quotes from Communist leaders themselves in their own publications. As far back as 1972, Gus Hall, a leader of the Communist Party USA, in his book, "A Lame Duck in Turbulent Waters," described what had been the long-time party policy:

"Our electoral policy has for 25 years been expressed in the phrase, 'the three legs of a stool'....The stool was constructed at a time when the Party was under sharp attack....a reflection of the Party's response to the difficulties. The flexibility was contained in the idea that no one leg of the stool was the main leg. Depending on the political pressures, one could choose a particular leg or legs. In fact the concept was built on the idea that when the other two legs, namely, the Communist Party and the forces of political independence, got strong enough, then and only then would the stool sit on three legs. But until that day comes the one operating leg would be the liberal wing of the Democratic Party." (Emphasis added.)

This is shocking but true. So the Communist Party and the "Forces of Political Independence" would operate within the Democratic Party until they were strong enough to break away from the Democratic Party and form a third independent Anti-Monopoly Peoples Party.

Hall, writing this in 1972, at that time claimed that he had decided the policy was wrong. It is apparent, however, from later quotes and actions of top Communists, including Hall, that the policy has in fact been continued and even augmented.

Gus Hall himself said at the time:

> **"We are going to work towards <u>independence</u>, but I think it is clear we are going to work with people who for some time will be 'riding two horses' in the field of political action."**

In other words, Hall is saying that the Communists will be working with people who are operating both as Democrats and as Communists.

In reading such quotes it is important to understand some of the Communists' key code words, sometimes called "fingerprint" words. "Forces of independence" sounds admirable, but in the Communist vocabulary this actually means those movements such as Labor, women's rights, gays, etc., who may now be operating within the Democratic Party, but who, the Communists hope, may later split off and become "independent" of the Democrats, and thus more amenable to backing Communist policies. Such large groups are already very helpful to Communist objectives.

Another common Communist phrase is "mass movements" or "movements of masses" referring to large groups such as Labor, which the Communists are continually trying to influence to promote their objectives.

A third important Communist code word is "progressive." Louis Budenz, former Editor of *The Daily Worker* and member of the Central Committee of the CPUSA, who later broke with the party, wrote the following in his book, "The Techniques of Communism":

> **"The Communist front is never referred to by that name in Red circles. In writing, any specific front is mentioned as 'a leading <u>progressive</u> organization'."**

It must be noted that not all progressives are Communists. They are often even more influential than Communists because they usually help the Communist causes.

Other Communist code words to apply to organizations being manipulated by or cooperating with the Party are "people's fronts" or "popular movements." Communist publications such as *The Daily World* and *Political Affairs* frequently refer to the "All People's Front" or "The All People's Unity" or the "Coalition of Independent Forces."

Proof of continuing Communist success in working through the Democratic Party can be shown by many more recent direct quotes from Communist Party officials. For example:

Charlene Mitchell, Executive Director of the Afro-American Commission of the CPUSA, writing in *The Daily World* June 9, 1983:

> **"To date, most of the debate has centered on the personalities of potential Black candidates and the pros and cons of such a challenge. The thrust of such a candidacy must be to develop the popular electoral base to prevent the <u>Democratic Party</u> from continuing its**

shift to the right and force a more <u>pro-gressive platform and program in the 1984 campaign</u>."

Another example, from the March 1989 issue of *Political Affairs*, the monthly publication of the CPUSA:

> "We see building political independence based on the alliance of labor with the African-American community as the aim for changing the relationship of forces in elected office. The Party Program maintains the ultimate expression of this would be a <u>mass anti-monopoly people's party</u>. . .

> "From the standpoint of process, even if it is currently <u>developing primarily through the Democratic Party</u>, the fact that labor, the Rainbow Coalition, and the African-American community are the main generators of the new developments substantiates our policy and our historic approach of basing the building of political <u>independence</u> on the alliance of the trade union movement and the African-American people. . .

> "Should the party strive to play a leading role helping those forces gain and consolidate new positions of strength, <u>even inside the Democratic Party</u> or shouldn't it?, I think it should.

> "How is our party going to develop its all-sided electoral presence? This cannot and should not repose solely on Communist or Left-independent candidates. Not if there is any intention of emerging as an <u>integral component of</u>

the overall progressive coalition, especially in view of the fact that the
Jackson-led progressive wing of the
Democratic Party is that coalition's major organized component."

In this same September/October 1988 issue,
Political Affairs states:

"Beyond the rhetoric, politics in
the United States invariably reflects the
class struggle. Even as parties of capitalism, the dynamics between and within
the Democratic and Republican parties
express the interests and demands of
competing sections of the ruling class,
on the one hand; and the cross-purposes
of contending class forces vying for control of the Democratic Party, on the
other.

"During the Reagan-Bush years
the Republican Party has become the
party of the ultra-Right. Organized
forces of the working class and people
are almost totally absent from it.

"For the last fifty years the
Democratic Party has housed a broad
mix of class and social forces that are
often in conflict with each other. This
has given rise to a sometimes subtle,
sometimes sharp struggle over direction. The status and intensity of this
struggle depend on the level and
strength of the political independence of
the labor movement and other people's
forces operating inside the (Democratic)
party." (Emphasis added.)

Another important example: *Political Affairs* for March 1989 contained the following statement:

> **"Organized mass movements— especially the African American community, the Rainbow Coalition, labor on all levels, SANE-Freeze, and other mass organizations—became more <u>independent of the Democratic Party establishment on policy and political direction, but more organizationally involved in the Democratic Party</u>."**

The same issue also contained the following:

> **"This much is clear – the overall movement will grow. So will the role of the Rainbow Coalition and the labor movement. And it will unfold in the 1989-1992 quadrennial cycle <u>primarily— but not exclusively—through the medium of the Democratic Party</u>."**

<u>CPLAN.</u> Communist publications also specifically describe a party apparatus for directly influencing the votes of Congress and even Congressional and Presidential Elections. This is called CPLAN, or the "Communist Party Legislative Action Network." This network has been organized to influence other mass organizations cooperating with the Communists through the "All Peoples Front" to stimulate telephone networks and letter writing campaigns to influence Congress on legislation and even to reach voters regarding election campaigns.

The May 1987 issue of *Political Affairs* describes CPLAN in more detail:

> **"(E)very party organization should assign a comrade to be in touch with the legislative and political action**

department of the Central Committee. This could be a key for rapid mobilization. The aim is to activate within a day or two all party organizations, as well as our mass movements connections, to pressure their Senators and Representatives. . .

"Nationally CPLAN would be able to generate tens of thousands of letters, telephone calls, mailgrams, etc....There are few questions on which CPLAN cannot make the difference in <u>how at least 5 to 10 Senators or Representatives would vote</u>. . .

"CPLAN is an important means of strengthening the unity of <u>the independent forces</u>, and this could have a great bearing not only on the 100th Congress but on the 1988 electoral struggle."(e.a.)

The same issue of *Political Affairs* also has this to say:

"When account is taken of the Party district and club organizations, as well as the thousands of trade unions, coalitions, and mass organizations on the grassroots, citywide, and national levels that Communists belong to, help lead, are active in, have friends, relatives, and contacts in, then the answer as to how to organize a Party legislative apparatus, as well as the Party's potential for influencing the legislative scene, become clear. . .the basis for an extraordinary legislative action network that could impact on the 100th Congress in a major way." (See Exhibits 1. & 2.)*

These are only a few of the many examples of Communist officials and publications frankly revealing their objectives of working through "mass organizations" and the "independent forces" to infiltrate and influence the liberal and "progressive" wings of the Democratic Party.

Note that all of the above evidence is given in the Communists' <u>own words</u>. These are direct quotes, not speculation based on second-hand evidence. This is definitely not "McCarthyism," personal charges based on unsubstantiated allegations.

The following chapters will outline in more detail how the Communists have been able to infiltrate the liberal wing of the Democratic Party, influence individual lawmakers, and manipulate the policies and votes of the Democratic party itself.

*Further details on CPLAN are given in "Gorbachev's Apparatus in the United States and 'The Moscow Spring'," Hearings of the National Committee to Restore Internal Security, in Washington, D.C. (Write Box 234, Mantoloking, N.J. 08738.), June 8, 1988.

Exhibit 1

What are some of the underlying factors stimulating deeper involvement in the legislative arena?

Millions upon millions of working people in factories and communities, on picket lines, farms, and campuses, are coming to the conclusion that fundamental solutions to their basic problems require action on a level exceeding struggle in a single shop, union, industry, farm, community, campus, city or state. Wide masses now know they can not fight for their day-to-day needs, let alone have an influence on such questions as the structural crisis, multinational corporations, democratic rights or arms control, without a viable legislative program. These problems require federal action. This realization is related to a growing understanding of the need for a Congress with a different kind of political composition, one that will undertake the new levels of action required to deal with these extraordinary problems.

WHEN ACCOUNT IS TAKEN of the Party district and club organizations as well as the thousands of trade unions, coalitions and mass organizations on the grassroots, citywide and national levels that Communists belong to, help lead, are active in, have friends, relatives and contacts in, then the answer as to how to organize a Party legislative apparatus as well as the Party's potential for influencing the legislative scene becomes clearer. The structures of the Party, its democratic centralist system of organization, its mass relationships, its extensive and intensive involvement in mass movements and struggles, its relationships with leaders and activists, constitute the basis for an extraordinary legislative action network that could impact on the 100th Congress in a major way.

Consider the implications of mobilizing our mass relationships and mass influence together with the Party organization per se around specific bills. Consider this particularly in light of the fact that we have Party organizations and members in close to 200 congressional districts and over 35 states. We have Party organizations in most of the states and congressional districts that are represented by chairs of key Senate and House committees and subcommittees, that are represented by most members of the Congressional Black Caucus, the Hispanic Caucus, the Arms Control Caucus, as well as other leading fighters on trade union issues, civil rights, economic justice, anti-apartheid solidarity, etc.

A Communist Party Legislative Action Network (CPLAN) could be an important means of helping strengthen the unity and cooperation of the independent forces on the national and especially the grassroots levels. This could have a great bearing not only on the 100th Congress but also the 1988 electoral struggles.

SHORT OF DESIGNATING a legislative director and establishing a district legislative or political action commission, every Party organization should assign a comrade to be in touch with the Legislative and Political Action Department of the Central Committee. This could be key for rapid mobilization. The aim is to activate, within a day or two, all Party organizations, as well as our mass-movement connections, to pressure their senators and representatives.

Nationally, CPLAN would be able to generate tens of thousands of letters, telephone calls, mailgrams, etc. CPLAN could help make the difference for millions of people between eating or starving, having decent housing or freezing to death in a cardboard box on some desolate sidewalk. It could help make the difference between keeping plants open and securing thousands of jobs, and entire cities being turned into ghost towns. It could help make the difference between imperialist intervention and national independence, between war and peace.

Are the possibilities being exaggerated? No, they aren't. In fact, there are numerous examples where precisely such questions have been decided by a handful of votes. Last year contra aid was approved by a half dozen votes in the Senate and less than a dozen in the House. One vote was the margin by which the last Congress increased Star Wars funding. There are few questions on which CPLAN could not make the difference in how at least 5 to 10 senators or representatives would vote.

Exhibit 2

Trade Union Work— Plus! The Communist Essence

GUS HALL

First, I want to commend the Trade Union Department for calling this conference. It is timely and necessary. It takes place at a very good moment for many reasons, including the fact that we are celebrating the 100th anniversary of May Day.

It is also timely in the sense that we are celebrating Reagan's first serious defeat—the vote in Congress against the $100 million for the Nicaraguan counterrevolutionaries. It is a tremendous victory and I think our Party acted quickly and more effectively than ever before on such an issue. The districts were already in gear when we called to check up.

I think the telephone has become the best, most effective and efficient method of protest in the country—surpassing petitions and delegations. It is a direct form of reaching opinionmakers. The calls are computerized and Congress gets the tally at the end of every day. But there's a wrinkle, which is new. Some congresspeople have been asking for names and addresses, which is a form of intimidation. However, many admitted it was the telephone campaign that changed their vote.

This conference is also timely because the congressional elections will be held in six months. It is possible that this election can spell the end of Reaganism.

It is also timely because it comes right on the heels of the 27th CPSU Congress, a congress that will have implications far, far beyond the borders of the Soviet Union.

It is timely because, come May 1, we will issue the first edition of the *People's Daily World*. Our new daily, national, working-class paper will raise our work to a new level. We should consider the new paper as a critical, indispensable instrument in the trade union field.

Opening and summary remarks by Gus Hall, general secretary, CPUSA at a Party conference on trade union work, March 22, 1986, at Unity Center, New York City.

This conference is timely because it comes after the Geneva Summit. There is now a danger of the collapse of the summit process. After the recent provocations there are some real obstacles to Summit II—the U.S. fleet violating the sea lanes of Libya, Bulgaria and the Soviet Union; the expulsion of Soviet personnel from the UN mission on the false charge of spying; the restrictions placed on the missions of Czechoslovakia, Bulgaria, the German Democratic Republic and Poland, and the most hostile, rabid and lying March 16 speech by Reagan.

It is especially timely because the Soviet Union proclaimed its last moratorium on nuclear testing on the basis that it will be in effect as long as the U.S. does not conduct another test. Today, almost at this very hour, a nuclear bomb will be tested in the Nevada desert, thus breaking the test ban. The ban will end as of today and then negotiations will have to start on a new basis.

The conference is timely because there has been a period of militant, long strikes, including those against Hormel, GE, American Can, TWA, Colt Industries, etc. These struggles raise some very important questions about our role. Generally, it was and is very positive, but with some negatives and weaknesses.

But above all else, it is timely because we meet after the 16th convention of the AFL-CIO. As we said at the last Central Committee meeting, that convention was more antimonopoly, antimultinational, antiracist, antiapartheid, politically independent and antidictatorship. Lane Kirkland has now included Chile in his denunciation of dictatorships, as well as commended the AFL-CIO for its support of the labor unions in the Philippines and its role in toppling Marcos. The convention was less anti-Communist, less class collaborationist.

This convention, which was the conver-

Chapter 3

Prominent Democrats with Communist Links

This chapter will summarize information on several leading Democrats, in and out of Congress, who have had close links with the Communist Party or its front groups during their careers. The large number of Democrats with such records is another strong indication of the success of the Communists in promoting their aims through this "third leg of the stool."

At the outset, we clearly state, we are not calling the following persons Communists. We are calling them Democrats.

Senator Howard Metzenbaum (D. Ohio).

Howard Metzenbaum was elected to the Ohio State House of Representatives in 1942 and to the Ohio Senate in 1947, where he served until 1951. He was elected to the U.S. Senate in 1973.

He served as the Secretary of the National Lawyers Guild (NLG). This organization was launched in 1936 as a spin-off of the International Labor Defense, a Communist front started in 1925 as the U.S. branch of the International Red Aid, a world-wide Soviet-backed group founded in 1922. (1)

In 1940, the NLG President, Russell N. Chase, was also the attorney for the Communist Party in Metzenbaum's home state of Ohio.

The NLG became affiliated in 1946 with the International Association of Democratic Lawyers (IADL), another Soviet front. Guild members have been prominent in Communist and far-left causes and organizations in the U.S. and have represented such far-left clients as the Weather Underground, SDS, the Cuban Government, atom spy Martin Sobell, Communist agent Judith Coplon, etc. One minor but significant detail is that the Guild's convention in Austin, Texas, in 1973 concluded with the singing of "The Internationale," the Communist anthem. And this song is no simple college pep song, as evidenced by its chorus:

> **"Tis the final conflict. Let each stand in his place. The International Soviet shall be the Human Race!"**

Metzenbaum was one of three "incorporators" of the Ohio School of Social Science in 1944 and later served as its Treasurer. This school was founded in Cleveland by the Communist Party to train operatives, recruit new party members, and "indoctrinate Communists and outsiders in the theory and practice of Communism," according to the Senate Internal Security Subcommittee. It was labeled "a Communist adjunct" by Tom Clark, Attorney General during the Truman Administration.

In recent years he has continued to be affiliated with pro-communist organizations. For example, in 1984 he was one of the "co-sponsors" of the Ninth Annual Banquet of the Labor Research Association (LRA). This organization has been identified as a Communist front, cooperating with the Soviet international front group, the World Federation of Trade Unions. The banquet honored

Democratic Congressman Charles Hayes. Other co-sponsors included Bella Abzug and actor Ed Asner.

Metzenbaum now serves on such sensitive committees as Intelligence, Judiciary (which has responsibility for FBI budgets and legislation), Energy and Natural Resources, and Labor and Human Resources. He consistently votes against a strong American defense. The American Security Council gave him a rating of 0% for 1988 (in contrast to 70% for his Democratic colleague from Ohio, John Glenn.)

Bella Abzug.

Mrs. Abzug was a prominent and vociferous left-wing Representative from New York City from 1970 to 1976 but lost a close bid to return to Congress in 1978.

She has more recently reappeared on the political scene by running for Chairperson of the Democratic National Committee's Women's Caucus. At the DNC's annual convention in September 1989, she lost to a moderate Democrat, Ruth Rudy of the Pennsylvania State Legislature, by a close vote of 81-80. She then contested the results, and in what some observers described as "a wild scene," she demanded a recount. As of January 1990, the dispute was still under "arbitration" within the DNC.

The fact that almost half of these Democratic women would vote for Bella is another indication of the leftist orientation of large elements of the Party. For Mrs. Abzug has a long history of pro-communist activities. Even in college she was notable for opposing American entry into World War II during the Hitler-Stalin pact, when Communists in this country were denouncing the war against Hitler. As soon as Hitler invaded Russia and the Communist Party made an abrupt shift in policy to support the war, Bella also flip-flopped to support it. This is a blatant ex-

ample of the behavior known as "zig-zag paral-
lelism," where an individual or organization makes
sudden radical shifts in direction that exactly parallel identical shifts in Communist policy, no matter
how sudden and irrational.

She joined the NLG and served on its Board of
Directors, as well as joining the International
Association of Democratic Lawyers, which has been
cited in State Department publications as a
Communist front. During the 1960s she became a
leader of Women Strike for Peace, which maintained
close relations with the Communist North
Vietnamese. In 1972 she went with a WSP delega-
tion to Paris to meet with Viet Cong and North
Vietnamese representatives. In a subsequent
Congressional hearing, 10 out of the 12 top officers
of WSP took the Fifth Amendment when asked about
Communist Party membership.

Bella Abzug opposed Hubert Humphrey's
presidential nomination in 1968 because she said he
had purged Communists in the Democratic-Farmer-
Labor Party in Minnesota.

While in Congress the record shows that she
never cast a vote in favor of national security. She
never made a single critical statement about
Communist tyranny, but during a debate on the Viet
Nam War she declared that Vietnamese and
Cambodian anti-communists should not be given
sanctuary in the U.S. in the event of a Communist
victory.

President Carter appointed her to head his
National Advisory Committee for Women, but had to
dismiss her six months later after she lectured him
shrilly before 40 other people at a Committee
meeting. Soon thereafter 23 other members of the
Committee resigned in sympathy, another indication
that radical viewpoints like Mrs. Abzug's have be-

come common in Democratic ranks. Now she has reappeared on the scene and has almost won the position of head of the Democrats' Women's Caucus. (2)

Charles A. Hayes.

Charles Hayes entered Congress for the first time in 1983. He won a special election to fill the seat vacated by Harold Washington for the First District of Illinois, which takes in part of Cook County, Chicago. It is a surprising fact that at the time of his nomination by the Democrats to run for this important seat, he was reported to be a long time member of the Communist Party. Whether he ever was or still is with the Communist Party, we personally do not know. This is probably the most extreme example of the Communists' success in using people who are "riding two horses." It is also another sign of the vulnerability of the Democratic Party to infiltration. (3)

Hayes won the regular election in 1984 and again in 1986, the latter by a margin of 96% to 4% over his Republican opponent, an indication of how safe this seat is for the Democrats.

He was 65 years old when first elected, an age when most men are retiring. He is now 71. Born in 1918 in Cairo, Illinois, when racial discrimination was still at its height, it is understandable why he developed a "progressive" point of view, but less understandable why he continues to follow or parallel some of the extreme left–wing policies of the Communist Party, supporting the totalitarian movements in Central America.

During the Depression he served in the Civilian Conservation Corps, the New Deal organization set up to give work to the unemployed. Later he became an active labor union leader, as Director, District 1, of the United Packinghouse Workers, and later International Vice President and Director of the United Food and Commercial Workers.

He was a co-founder and later Vice President of Operation PUSH, Jesse Jackson's organization that was organized to promote minority businesses.

He is a member of the Congressional Black Caucus, and has voted consistently with this group in opposing aid to the non-communists in Central America. For example, in 1989 he voted in favor of the following measures supporting the Communist efforts in El Salvador:

– House Concurrent Resolution 1 to slash military aid to El Salvador.

– Concurrent Resolution 48 "Expressing the Sense of the Congress that the United States Should Pursue a Negotiated Settlement to the Civil War in El Salvador." This was introduced by Nancy Pelosi (CA) just as the Salvadoran Communists had started a new call for negotiations and demands that the 1989 Presidential election be postponed.

– Joint Resolution 54, introduced by Robert Kastenmeier, to ban military aid to El Salvador completely.

Hayes was given a rating of 0% for 1988 by the American Security Council.

Alan Cranston

Cranston is the senior Senator from California, serving in the Senate since 1969. He is now also the Majority Whip, having been elected Democratic Whip in 1977.

This influential Senator from the third largest state has a consistent record of voting against almost all aid to countries fighting Communist aggression or insurgencies, including South Viet Nam and El Salvador, and for refusing to support anti-communist movements fighting for democracy in Communist dictatorships like Nicaragua, Angola, Mozambique etc. His 1988 American Security Council rating was 0%.

During his career he has also taken many actions that are even more directly favorable to Communist causes. In World War II he was Chief of the Foreign Language Division of the Office of War Information, the U.S. information and propaganda organization. In this position he made several surprisingly pro-communist moves.

For example, he recommended that the OWI hire one David Karr, as "a senior liaison officer working with other Federal agencies." Karr had been writing for the Communist newspaper, *The Daily Worker*, as well as for Albert Kahn, an author who was later revealed in Congressional testimony to be a Soviet agent.

In spite of this record, Cranston recommended Karr for employment, claiming that he knew he had worked for *The Daily Worker* but did not know he was a Communist! (Only Communists and non-communist helpers of Communism work for this Communist newspaper, now called *The Daily World*.)

After the War Karr launched a successful career in international finance and became even more active in pro-communist work. In 1975, for example, he arranged a $250 million credit for the Soviet Foreign Trade Bank. His main contact in Moscow was reported to be Jermen Gvishiani, deputy chairman of the Soviet State Committee for Science and

Technology and nephew of Soviet Premier Kosygin. Karr was also active in a campaign to have a defector from Communism, Richard Krebs, deported. Krebs had been a functionary of the German Communist Party but defected and wrote a dramatic expose of Communism and Fascism, "Out of the Night" under the pen name, Jan Valtin, published in 1941. One of Karr's last deals before his death in 1979 was the sale of Soviet Olympic gold coins in cooperation with Occidental Petroleum, whose chairman is Armand Hammer, the well known pro-Soviet industrialist.

Nevertheless, Cranston remained a friend of Karr and said later that Karr "had a strong social conscience that made him an intense promoter of Detente." (4)

While with the OWI in World War II, Cranston had also made other statements paralleling the Communist line. One concerned the assassination of Carlos Tresca in 1943. Tresca had been an Italian Communist, but broke with the party and became an intense opponent of the Stalinists and was allied with the Anarchists. He was gunned down in New York City in January 1943. His widow and friends said he had been slain because of his refusal to enter into a United Front with the Communists. Alan Cranston, however, issued a statement as an OWI official that Tresca had not opposed the Communists in a United Front organization, the Victory Council.

Throughout his career in the Senate, Cranston has been one of the most radical in opposing aid to countries fighting Communist insurgencies like South Viet Nam and El Salvador, and for refusing to support anti-communist movements fighting for democracy in Communist dictatorships like Nicaragua, Angola, Mozambique etc.

During the 1988 Presidential primaries when he was one of the Democratic contenders, he continued to show this tendency.

For example, during the New Hampshire primary he took part in a forum for all the candidates moderated by Barbara Walters. There were many reports at that time about the growing economic crisis in Mexico and increasing evidence of Communist agitation and subversion encouraged by Castro's Cuba. Walters asked each candidate about what his reaction would be to a Communist takeover in Mexico. Cranston refused to be alarmed by the prospect and instead switched to a criticism of U.S. policy toward the hard-pressed anti-communist government of El Salvador. "We have backed tyrants or even imposed tyrants on other people," he said. "The Mexican government is telling the U.S. to stop what you're doing in El Salvador, stop backing the tyranny there, stop trying to overthrow the government of Nicaragua, and we will be able to take care of our problems." (5)

In fact the U.S. policy on Nicaragua was simply to back what the people of Nicaragua wanted–Democracy.

Jesse Jackson

One of the front runners for the Democratic nomination for President in 1984 and 1988, Jesse Jackson ended second only to Michael Dukakis in 1988, and was plainly disappointed not to be picked as Dukakis's Vice Presidential running mate. This successful Democrat has probably displayed more pro-communist actions and associations than any other Democratic candidate in recent years. A few examples:

– A principal advisor to Jackson for more than 20 years has been Hunter Pitts O'Dell. O'Dell assisted

Jackson during his campaign for the Presidential
nomination. He was International Affairs Director for
Jackson's Operation PUSH in Chicago from the early
1960s onwards, and later for Jackson's Rainbow
Coalition, where he now serves.

It was reported that O'Dell had a long record
as a prominent and active member of the Communist
Party. During the 1950s, he was the head organizer
for the Communist Party USA in the South. In the
1960s he became an advisor to Martin Luther King
Jr. He was simultaneously serving on the National
Committee of the CPUSA under the pseudonym of
"Cornelius James." Several witnesses   before   the
Senate Internal Security Committee testified about
his activities. (6)

King's relations with O'Dell and other
Communists were major factors in causing President
John Kennedy and his brother, Robert, the Attorney
General, to approve an investigation of King by the
FBI.   Jack and Bobby Kennedy warned King about
O'Dell and other Communist associates. King then
claimed to have fired O'Dell but O'Dell later turned
up as head of King's organization in New York City.
After King's assassination, O'Dell began to work for
Jesse Jackson under the name Jack O'Dell.

O'Dell is also a member of the World Peace
Council, characterized by the CIA and the State
Department as an international Communist front.
Dee Bates of Jackson's Operation PUSH is a member
of the U.S. Peace Council, the America affiliate of this
front. In spite of this long record of Communist
links, O'Dell still denies that he was a member of the
party. For the record, we do not know whether he is
or was a Communist.

– Another prominent Jackson aide is Mary
Tate, also a leading member of the World Peace
Council. Tate went with Jackson to Damascus, Syria,

in 1983 to negotiate for the release of U.S. Navy Lieutenant Robert Goodman, who had been shot down and imprisoned by the Syrians. Some observers believe this episode had been simply planned in advance by the Jackson staff and the pro-communist Syrians as a way of embarrassing Reagan. Syria helped pay for some expenses of the trip. (7)

Jackson's other pro-communist actions include:

–In June and July 1984 during his presidential campaign he toured Cuba and Nicaragua partly at those governments' expense, praising Castro and the Sandinistas and the Salvadorean Communist guerillas, and being photographed embracing Castro. Actions speak louder than words.

– He and several other prominent Democrats have supported CISPES (The Committee in Solidarity with the People of El Salvador). This is an organization with affiliates in more than 300 U.S. cities and university campuses. It supports the Communist guerillas in El Salvador. Documents captured in a Salvador safe house by the Salvador Army and published by the U.S. State Department revealed that CISPES is a Communist front organized by a Salvador Communist agent visiting the U.S. in 1980. Yet Jackson continues to support CISPES.

– Jackson has shown consistent support for the terrorist Palestine Liberation Organization and Yasar Arafat. In 1984 he and two Democratic Congressmen, John Conyers and George Crockett, were among the signers of a telegram sent by a PLO support group to President Reagan demanding "immediate sanctions against Israel." (8)

– He was a supporter of the Communist regime in Grenada before the U.S. organized the liberation of that island. Dessima Williams, the ambassador of that

regime in Washington, remained in this country following the liberation long after her diplomatic visa
had expired, stirring up opposition to U.S.
"militarism." The INS finally arrested her and
ordered her deportation. Jackson's wife, Jacqueline,
then offered to take her into personal custody. (9)

There are many signs of Communist involvement in the formation and continuing operations of
Jackson's Operation PUSH and Rainbow Coalition.
The Communist *Daily World* said on April 13, 1984
during the Presidential primaries:

> **"The answer to Reagan and Bush is to
> redouble efforts to build and strengthen
> the all peoples' front, a vital part of
> which is the campaign being waged on
> the issues by Jesse Jackson." (e.a.)**

Here we see another example of the
Communists' use of the phrase, "all people's front"
to describe a joint operation between the Party and
sometimes unwitting collaborators.

Communist Party vice presidential candidate
Angela Davis added:

> **"The Jesse Jackson campaign is go-
> ing to force the Democratic Party to
> speak on issues that they ordinarily
> would not address."**

Former Black Panther Eldridge Cleaver, who
broke with the Panthers and became an active anti-
Communist after experiences in Cuba and pro-communist countries in North Africa and Eastern
Europe, says that the Rainbow Coalition has roots in
the Black Panther movement. He says it uses simply
"warmed over" 1960s Panther rhetoric, even including its name. Old Panther newspapers, he points out,

refer to a "rainbow coalition" of blacks, whites, and Puerto Ricans.

A strong supporter of the Rainbow Coalition is the Workers World Party (WWP), an extreme Communist group that advocates terrorism and has had links with the violent Weather Underground. The WWP backed Jackson and the Rainbow Coalition in 1984 through one of its fronts, the All Peoples' Congress.

The Communist Party USA also backed Jackson's candidacy in 1984. Their publications like *The Daily World* gave Jackson more coverage than even the Party's own candidates, Gus Hall and Angela Davis. Jackson never repudiated this Communist support.

Libyan Dictator Moammar Quadaffi is a close friend and admirer of Jackson. He has helped to fund some of Jackson's projects including Operation PUSH. He and Jackson are both friends of the radical Louis Farrakhan and his anti-Semitic violence-prone Nation of Islam. Quadaffi has boasted that he has the ability to bring terrorism into the United States. (10)

Jackson never repudiated Farrakhan's support during the 1988 campaign although he was frequently asked about it.

Jackson continues to have a major influence on the Democratic Party. His effective campaigning has undoubtedly made it more possible for Blacks to run for high office. The recent election victories of David Dinkins in New York City and Douglas Wilder in Virginia (the first Black to be elected a State governor) have been partly ascribed to Jackson's past work in making Black political prominence more feasible.

Wilder, however, made an effort to distance himself from Jackson and never invited him into Virginia to help his campaign. Dinkins did the same in New York City. Both candidates recognized that Jackson's radicalism might scare off many voters. Yet on the night of his election victory, Dinkins suddenly made a flattering reference to Jackson in a speech, thus showing that he is more favorable to Jackson's radical viewpoints than he had admitted during his campaign.

Gus Hall, when asked who the Communist Party would support for President in the 1988 election, said:

"As a political party we do not endorse candidates of other political parties. Communists as individuals work in the election campaign, even in the campaigns of other candidates, not only Communist candidates.

"I think our members will work for the candidates they think have the most progressive, most advanced positions. At this stage most members of the Party will be working for Jesse Jackson on the basis that he does have an advanced position. But we do not endorse any candidate, including Jackson."

If you keep in mind that Communist Party members are "under discipline," which means they cannot engage in any activities, especially political work, without the approval or even the direct orders of the Party, it seems obvious that any work assisting Jackson's campaign is with the approval or orders of the Party.

Ronald Brown

Ron Brown was elected to the key position of Chairman of the Democratic National Committee in February 1989 as the Party was attempting to rebuild its national structure after the Dukakis defeat. Brown himself had worked extensively for Jesse Jackson, so he presumably shares many of the same radical political ideas.

The Communist Party welcomed Brown's election. The *People's Daily World* commented as follows:

"BROWN'S DNC ELECTION PART OF ONGOING STRUGGLES"

"Ronald Brown's election by acclamation as Chair of the Democratic National Committee last Friday was a big step forward for all-people's unity against reaction.

"It reflected the strength of the Labor/African-American alliance and the unprecedented impact of the Rev. Jesse Jackson's 1988 presidential campaign. Also swept into office to head the DNC was a multi-racial leadership which included three women, a labor representative, a second African-American and a Latino.

"Brown, and the team at the DNC which was elected to help him, reflect the strength of all-people's unity against Reaganite reaction. . .

The past shows that Brown's election is part of a process in which people's united forces for progress have been using the Democratic Party as one of their

vehicles. How far that process goes will
be determined by the outcome of clashes
between the people's forces inside and
outside the Democratic Party and the
forces of monopoly capital inside and
outside the Democratic Party. (Emphasis
added. Note the Communist code words,
"people's united forces" and "people's
forces," indicating Communist joint operations.) (11)

Brown's election to Chairman of the
Democratic National committee could be interpreted
as how close the Communist Party and its non-
communist helpers are to taking over the leadership
of the Democratic Party.

Anne Braden

Anne Braden has been active in Democratic
politics for many years. She was a delegate to the
Democratic Nominating Convention in 1980 and an
alternate delegate in 1984. At the same time, she
has been a member of the Communist Party, another
good example of the party utilizing "two legs of a
stool." She was a CPUSA organizer and from 1970
onwards she was Executive Director of the Southern
Conference Education Fund, an organization with
several Communists in its leadership and dedicated
to promoting racial integration "by revolutionary
means."

She was placed on the November 1988 presidential ballot in Kentucky as an elector for the
CPUSA ticket of Gus Hall.

She was also a member of the National Council
of the National Emergency Civil Liberties Committee
(NECLC), cited as a Communist front by the House
Un-American Activities Committee. This Council has
included such identified Communists on its Board as

Frank Wilkinson, Harvey O'Connor, Victor Rabinowitz, and Jonathan Lubell.

(Frank Wilkinson was long associated with Ann Braden's husband, Carl, and both were cited as Communists at the same time by the House UnAmerican Activities Committee.)

The NECLC has given legal assistance to many Communists or Communist causes including the Soviet agent, Judith Coplon, and the Castro government of Cuba. (12)

Regarding her being a delegate to the 1984 Democratic Convention, Mrs. Braden stated that a Black delegate had been elected to vote for Jesse Jackson at the Convention but local Black politicians awarded it to her "to further the cause of coalition-building," another example of the Democratic Party cooperating with Communists to further a coalition.(13)

George W. Crockett Jr.

George Crockett is an influential Democratic Congressman from Detroit, Michigan. He is a member of the important Judiciary and Foreign Affairs committees. On the latter he was elevated in 1987 to Chairman of the Subcommittee on Western Hemisphere Affairs, which has jurisdiction over the vital and controversial area of Central America.

Crockett has a long record of pro-communist affiliations, including the following:

– In the 1940s he was a law partner of Maurice Sugar, who had been expelled from the United Auto Workers by Walter Reuther for being a Communist.

– He joined the National Lawyers Guild and later became a Vice President. He is still a member.

– In 1946 he was a sponsor of the Civil Rights Congress, cited before Congressional committees as a Communist front.

– In 1949 he was a legal counsel for the 11 Communist Party officials, including Gus Hall, accused of advocating the overthrow of the U.S. government by force. These leaders were convicted and sentenced to jail, and Crockett himself was sentenced to four months in jail for contempt of court because of his disruptive behavior during the trial.

– In 1952 and 1954 he represented Communist witnesses before the House Un-American Activities Committee, (which had a Democratic majority), and was admonished several times by the Committee counsel for his conduct.

– He sponsored a reception in support of Julius and Ethel Rosenberg, then in prison awaiting execution for transmitting atomic bomb secrets to the Soviets.

– After the Soviets shot down the Korean Airline Flight 007 in 1983 with the death of many civilians including Congressman Lawrence MacDonald, Crockett was one of only two Congressmen to abstain on a House resolution condemning the Soviets. The resolution passed by 416 to 0.

– In 1985 he explicitly defended the Soviets on the House floor in a debate over a resolution condemning the Soviets for the killing of Major Arthur Nicholson in Germany. He then voted against the resolution.

– He has never publicly admitted membership in the Party, but the radical New York Civil Rights Congress once described him as one of several "former Communist political prisoners." We leave it to you, the reader, to judge whether he has been a Communist or a non-communist helper of Communism.

As chairman of the important House Subcommittee on Western Hemisphere Affairs, Crockett has great influence on House policy in this controversial area, including Central America. He is authorized to see a large volume of highly classified information about developments there.

Crockett won out for this chairmanship over Congressman Dan Mica of Florida. Mica had seniority on the Foreign Affairs Committee and wanted the job, but he had voted for aid to the Nicaraguan Freedom Fighters, an anti-communist stance that resulted in his losing out to Crockett. The fact that the Democrats would prefer a man with Crockett's procommunist background for this sensitive post says a lot about the current influence of the Communists and their non-communist helpers on the Democratic leadership. (14)

John Conyers Jr.

Crockett's fellow Congressman from Detroit, John Conyers, may have a less extensive background of Communist affiliations, but he has shown an equally pro-communist record since his election to Congress in 1965. A few examples:

– He has consistently supported the activities of the World Peace Council and the U.S. Peace Council, cited in several FBI and State Department publications as Communist fronts that concentrate on undermining the U.S. defense effort and justifying the Soviet arms build up.

In 1978 the CPUSA and other radical groups formed a National Committee to welcome to Washington a WPC delegation and its President,

Romesch Chandra, a member of the Communist
Party of India. Conyers welcomed this group, saying
"You have joined us to give courage and inspiration
in our fight for disarmament and against the neutron
bomb."

In 1981 another WPC delegation led by
Chandra toured the U.S. to publicize the "nuclear
freeze" then being promoted by Leonid Brezhnev.
This group met with several Congressmen at the
Capitol, including Conyers, Crockett, Ron Dellums,
Don Edwards, and other Democrats.

In 1982 the House Intelligence Committee
prepared a report on the pro-Soviet activities of the
World Peace Council. The committee staff, under the
direction of Representative Edward Boland (D.
Mass.), doctored the report to remove the names of
six Congressmen who had participated in WPC meetings. These included Conyers, Dellums, Rangel,
Dymally, Leland, and Edwards himself. (15)

– He has consistently voted against every new
U.S. weapons program and opposed the defense
budgets. The American Security Council rated him at
0% for 1988.

<u>Ronald V. Dellums</u>

Ron Dellums, representing the ultra-liberal
Berkeley district of California since 1971, has shown
one of the most radical records of any Congressman.
He emerged in the 1960s as a left–wing activist in
California, often appearing as a rabble-rousing
speaker at Black Panther rallies.

After being elected to Congress in 1970, he
moderated his rhetoric somewhat and began to
adopt more of a purely "liberal" pose. His voting
record and other actions while in Congress,
however, show a consistent pattern of radical actions

that benefit causes approved by the Communists. A few of the most blatant examples:

– Soon after his election in 1970 Dellums flew to Helsinki for a meeting of the World Peace Council, well identified as a Communist front, where numerous resolutions were passed attacking the U.S. as "an enemy of peace." On his return he opened an exhibit in the House Office Building of photos of alleged U.S. atrocities in Vietnam splashed with artificial blood.

– In 1980, the Salvadoran Communists, engaged in a guerilla war with their government, sent an agent to the United States, Shafik Handal, brother of the Party chairman, Farid Handal. His mission was to organize a nationwide front group to support the guerillas. After meeting with the Cuban Communist UN Mission and the CPUSA "Solidarity Coordinator," Sandy Pollack, in New York, Handal went to Washington. There he was put in touch with Dellums, who provided him with office space and it was arranged for him to meet with the Congressional Black Caucus.

Handal later reported that:

"The offices of Congressman Dellums were turned into our offices. Everything was done there. The meeting with the Black Caucus took place in the belly of the monster himself, nothing less than in the meeting room of the House Foreign Affairs Committee."

Handal and his American collaborators then organized the Committee in Solidarity with the People of El Salvador, or CISPES, which now has branches in 300 cities and universities across the country. CISPES consistently supports the Salvadoran Communists, agitating against aid to the hard-pressed democratically elected government, and joining in demonstrations against aid to the anti-Communist Freedom Fighters in Nicaragua.

– Later the Salvadoran Communist Radio Venceremos announced:

> **"We have organized a large soli-darity apparatus that encompasses the whole planet, even in the United States, where one of the most active centers of solidarity exists." (16)**

– In April 1980, referring to the Soviet invasion of Afghanistan, Dellums wrote his constituents that the real tragedy of that action was that it has "provided an excuse for U.S. intervention in the internal affairs of Pakistan on the pretext of aiding the Afghan rebels." (The Afghan "rebels" were in fact fighting against a puppet regime imposed by the Soviet Union for their own strategic purposes.)

– Dellums is a regular attendee at World and U.S. Peace Council events, well identified as Communist fronts. On December 15, 1981, for example, Dellum's assistant, Barbara Lee, wrote to the WPC asking for airline tickets and hotel accommodations for Dellums and two staff members to attend the WPC Conference in Vienna. The letter was addressed to Karen Talbot, an American working for the WPC in Helsinki. Talbot was formerly business manager of *People's World*, the Communist Party USA newspaper, published in Dellums' district.(17)

– He works closely with the far left think tank, the Institute for Policy Studies. He has taught courses at the Washington School, run by IPS, and was on the committee and a speaker at the IPS 20th Anniversary celebration in 1984. In 1983 he published a book, "Defense Sense: The Search for a Rational Military Policy," a collection of papers prepared for Congressional hearings sponsored by

Dellums on "alternative" defense budgets. Contributors included four top officers of IPS. (18)

– His Congressional staffers along with those of Conyers launched the Progressive Hill Staff Group, made up of aides to left–wing Congressmen. Among other actions this group was active in the trend for Congress to short circuit the State Department on Foreign Affairs. They organized a conference in 1983 for three members of the Communist Sandinista government of Nicaragua to address more than 100 Congressional staffers and press reporters on Capitol Hill. The State Department was given no advance notice of the meeting. This helped the cause of Communism in Nicaragua in your Congress.

– Dellums is a prominent member of the House Armed Services Committee where he has access to large amounts of classified information and regularly opposes defense projects. After the Soviets invaded Afghanistan and Jimmy Carter tried to increase the Defense Budget, Dellums opposed, saying he was alarmed by the idea of American "militarism." He remains silent on Soviet "militarism."

– He was an admirer and supporter of Maurice Bishop, the Communist dictator of Grenada. Dellums' assistant, Carlotta Scott, wrote to Bishop as follows,

> "Ron has become truly committed to Grenada. . .and doesn't want anything to happen to building the Revolution and making it strong. . .He really admires you as a. . .leader with courage and foresight, principles and integrity. . .The only other person I know of that he expresses such admiration for is Fidel."

During the 1988 campaign Dellums became a prominent adviser on Defense to Jesse Jackson. This is another indication of the growing influence of pro-

communists in the higher echelons of the
Democratic Party. (See the startling information on
Dellums at the end of this book.)

Edward Asner.

A long time leader of radical causes, for years
he knowingly or unknowingly paralleled the
Communist line. Because of Communism's
unpopularity in the Soviet Union, he is following the
same old radical line, but changing the name.

The Communist Party is the only party in the
Soviet Union. However, remember that the U.S.S.R.
officially is the Union of Soviet Socialist Republics.
Russia is actually a Socialist state—not a Communist
state. It is, however, run by the Communist Party.
Confusing, but designed that way by the Communists
so they can call themselves either Communists or
Socialists whenever they choose to do so.

Ed Asner has now affiliated himself with the
organization, Democratic Socialists of America (DSA).
This, of course, promotes many policies similar to
those of the U.S.S.R. Nothing has changed but the
name. Remember that Socialism, wherever it is,
does not work and has not worked for 70 years in
the Union of Soviet Socialist Republics. It would
never work in the United States, but followers of the
failed Socialist system in Russia are now trying to put
Socialism in place in the United States.

In his fund raising letter of May 1990, on
Democrtic Socialism stationery, Asner states:

> "Arbitrary power in the East has
> met its match and has been relegated to
> the dustbin of history by the power of the
> people. Arbitrary power in America has
> not. In America that arbitrary power has
> a name: capitalism."

Asner is against capitalism, which is your economic system. He is for a socialist system that has failed in Russia. He now points to Sweden where socialism is also failing.

He further states:

> "DSA believes in a fundamental redistribution of wealth and power in this country. . .Join with progressive public officials like Congressman Ron Dellums and San Francisco City Supervisor Harry Britt. . .who are working through DSA to bring together the day-to-day battles for social change with the longer-term strategies and visions. Your contribution of $20, $35, $50, $100 or more will make you a "card-carrying" democratic socialist. It will push forward the work of promoting democratic socialist alternatives <u>and</u> building a progressive majority in the Nineties."

Refer to the Glossary for the definition of the word "progressive" which follows: Used by Communists to denote people or organizations that are pro-communist, or promoting a Communist line. (Many people calling themselves "progressive" are not Communists but may unwittingly aid the Communists.)

And beware of joining any "Democratic Socialist" organization. It is the wolf in sheep's clothing. It is a new name for the same old Socialist theory that for seventy years has failed. Some people cannot admit they were wrong, and seek new names for the same old Socialist garbage.

"The Congressional Pink Caucus"

In October 1989 the Sandinista Government caused a shock even among American liberals by announcing that they would no longer comply with the 19 month-old cease-fire agreement with the Contras. This had been considered a prime step forward for the "peace process" that was progressing slowly as part of the Arias Peace Plan.

A resolution was introduced in Congress deploring the Sandinistas' action. The Senate voted unanimously in favor, but in the House the vote was 379-29. All the 29 Congressmen voting against the resolution were Democrats. The Council for Inter-American Security calls these people "The Congressional Pink Caucus", they were unknowingly paralleling the Communist line:

Jim Bates (CA)	Robt. Kastenmeier (WI)
Barbara Boxer (CA)	John Lewis (GA)
William Clay (MO)	Major Owens (NY)
George Crockett (MI)	Nancy Pelosi (CA)
Cardiss Collins (IL)	Charles Rangel (NY)
Peter DeFazio (OR)	Gus Savage (IL)
Ronald Dellums (CA)	Louis Stokes (OH)
Mervyn Dymally (CA)	Gerry Studds (MA)
Don Edwards (CA)	Esteban Torres (CA)
Lane Evans (IL)	Adolphus Towns (NY)
Floyd Flake (NY)	Jolene Unsoeld (WA)
Henry Gonzalez (TX)	Ted Weiss (NY)
Charles Hayes (IL)	Alan Wheat (MO)
Joseph Kennedy (MA)	Ron Wyden (OR)
Peter Kostmayer (PA)	

A Note on Racism.

Many Democrats named in this book are Blacks or other minorities. For this reason, "progressives" may hurl charges of racism against me. This is not the case. I am not a racist nor have I ever been. In fact many years ago in the 1940s, during an early job with the Federal Government, I was a major player in helping the entire Black Movement break the salary barrier. (Of course it was not called the Black Movement in those days.)

In my job in the War Production Board in the early 1940s, I employed two Black women in a grade higher than CAF-1, which had a salary limit of $1,280 per year. There was an unwritten law among white administrative officers that no Black woman was to be hired above CAF-1 at $1,280 nor a Black man above that of Messenger, also at $1,280.

I employed two Black women as Clerks, CAF-2, at $1,440 annually, a grade above the unwritten law. I was first fired "with prejudice." After a hearing at my request where I was defended by the top lawyers of the National Association for the Advancement of Colored People, I proved racism existed in the Agency and was cleared of all charges.

However, I was still fired, but "without prejudice." I was called a Communist, which I was not, and told I would be forever "blackballed" from a government job. I was without work for over a year. When I told my story to Edward R. Stettinius Jr., former Secretary of State, he praised my stand and hired me on the spot.

So when I criticize individual Blacks, I am not criticizing them as Blacks for their race but on ideological grounds. In this book I have criticized equally both Whites and Blacks for being Communists, "progressives," members of "the forces of independence," and helpers of Communism. No racism is involved.

NOTES

1.   A summary of evidence from Congressional committees on the NLG as a Soviet front is given in "Protecting Traitors, Spies, and Terrorists," Church League of America, Wheaton, Ill., 1977.
2. *Human Events*, October 7, 1989, p.3.
3. Hayes' membership in the Party is described in House Committee on UnAmerican Activities hearings: "Communist Activities in the Chicago Area," Part 2, p.3767, 1952; "Communist Penetration of Vital Industries - Chicago," p.583-4, 1959. Cited in John A. Stormer, *None Dare Call It Treason - 25 Years Later*, Liberty Bell Press, Florissant, Mo.,1990, p. 277, 389.
4.   House Special Committee on Un-American Activities, Vol.7, 3383 ff.; *Business Week*, May 19, 1975, p.2, and *Fortune*, December 3, 1979 p.94; all summarized in Herbert Romerstein and Stanislav Levchenko, *The KGB Against the Main Enemy*, Lexington Books, Lexington, Mass. 1989. p.122.
5. New Hampshire Democratic Forum, 23 February 1984, quoted in Allan C. Brownfeld and J. Michael Waller, *The Revolution Lobby, Council for Inter-American Security*, Washington, 1985, p. 60.
6. *Information Digest*, April 3, 1987, p.69.
7. Brownfeld and Waller, p. 96.
8. Palestine Congress in North America telegram quoted in Brownfeld and Waller, op.cit.,p.41.
9. Brownfeld and Waller, p. 73.
10. *U.S. News and World Report*, June 25, 1984, quoted in Brownfeld and Waller, op.cit. p.97.
11. *People's Daily World*, February 15, 1989.
12.   House Internal Security Committee reports summarized in *Protecting Traitors, Spies, and Terrorists*, Church League of America, Wheaton, Ill., 1977.
13. *Information Digest*. November 2, 1984.

14. These facts on Crockett's background are summarized from "Congress's Red Army" by J.Michael Waller and Joseph Sobran, *National Review*, July 31, 1987; and "Direct Communist Influence on U.S. Congress Growing Dramatically," by Allan C. Brownfeld, *Human Events*, October 31, 1987.
15. Ibid.
16. Brownfeld & Waller, p. 32 ff.
17. Allan C. Brownfeld, "Direct Communist Influence on U.S. Congress Growing Dramatically," *Human Events*, 10/31/87 p.23. 18. Ibid.

Chapter 4

Democrats Cooperating with Communist Front Groups

The U.S. Communist Party is not the only conduit through which the Communists have been manipulating the Democratic Party. The Soviet Union and its satellites also work directly through various international front groups and their American branches.

Raymond Wannall, former chief of the FBI's Counter Intelligence service, says that since the 1950s, Soviet propaganda and subversion in the U.S. have been increasingly directed from outside the country, with the CPUSA playing only a subsidiary role.

Such propaganda activities are directed by the International Department of the Communist Party of the Soviet Union, with the KGB responsible for much of the implementation. Americans are recruited to work for this propaganda effort either by Soviet agents approaching sympathetic Americans abroad, or by Soviet agents working within the U.S. KGB personnel assigned to recruiting and controlling Americans for propaganda or subversive purposes are known as "Line PR" agents. Such Soviet control officers can travel in and out of the U.S. without much restriction.

In 1986 the U.S. expelled 80 Soviet nationals employed at the UN and the Soviet embassy because they had been working as Line PR agents, control officers for American citizens serving as "agents of influence in the American media or government." (1)

The Communists use a number of pretexts and vehicles for recruiting people to cooperate with their campaigns. Among the most important are front groups.

Lenin was the first Communist leader to stress the importance of creating or infiltrating organizations that could recruit large numbers of non-communists to promote Communist objectives. He and his followers preached the necessity to promote such fronts to expand greatly the Communists' ability to mobilize wide support among masses of people who might not otherwise agree with Communist aims.

The Soviet Union has vigorously followed this policy. A large number of international fronts have been built up over the years. Since World War II they have proliferated widely, mainly directed against the defense efforts of the U.S. and other democracies in the name of "peace," or with other objectives in line with Communist aims.

In October 1987 the State Department published a long report on "Soviet Influence Activities: A Report on Active Measures and Propaganda, 1986-87." This was written with the cooperation of the CIA, U.S. Information Agency, Arms Control and Disarmament Agency, Defense Intelligence Agency, and the Departments of Defense and Justice. The FBI contributed a chapter on Active Measures within the U.S.

This report summarized the latest information on the leading Soviet fronts and their U.S. branches. Among these the most important with their American affiliates are the following:

Women's International Democratic Federation	Women Strike for Peace
International Assoc. of Democratic Lawyers	National Lawyers Guild
World Federation of Trade Unions	Trade Unions For Action & Democracy/ Labor Research Assoc.

The U.S. Communist Party has taken part in this front effort even though it is not the main channel. Communist publications in the U.S. frequently speak of the need to use "mass organizations" to mobilize large numbers of non-communists behind the Party's causes. And much of this is being done through the Democratic Party. In March 1989, for example, the U.S. Communist Party journal, *Political Affairs*, wrote:

> "Organized mass movements – especially the African American community, the Rainbow Coalition, labor on all levels, SANE-Freeze, and other mass organizations – become more independent of the Democratic Party establishment on policy and in political direction, but more organizationally involved in the Democratic Party."

Prominent members of the Democratic Party have been active in a number of the groups identified as Communist fronts in the State Department report

and other government documents. Most notable of
these fronts are the following:

The World Peace Council

In 1949 the World Peace Council (WPC) was
founded in Prague during a "Peace Congress" sponsored by the Soviets and their Czech and other
Eastern European satellites. The organization was
planned and controlled by the International
Department of the Communist Party of the Soviet
Union (CPSU). It claimed to represent 600 million
"organizers for peace" around the world, but was
soon recognized by knowledgeable observers as no
more than a Soviet front.

In 1978 the House Intelligence Committee
released a large CIA report on Soviet propaganda and
front groups around the world (outside the U.S.) in
which the WPC was identified as such a front. It has
continued to be so identified in other government
reports including State Department documents. (2)

In 1981 the WPC applied for Consultative
Status with the UN Economic and Social Council, but
withdrew its application when required to submit
audited financial statements. (3)

After being expelled from several countries,
the WPC finally set up headquarters in Helsinki. It is
now estimated to have an annual budget of more than
$40 million, almost all provided by the USSR. It
consistently supports Soviet foreign policy and attacks the defense efforts of the U.S. and the other
democracies.

In spite of such clear exposure of the WPC as a
Soviet tool, several Democratic members of Congress
have been active supporters for many years.

For example, in 1978 the U.S. Communist Party formed a "National Committee" to welcome the President of the WPC to Washington for a "Dialogue on Disarmament and Detente." This President was Romesch Chandra, a well known member of the Communist Party of India. Others attending from overseas included KGB Colonel Radomir Bogdanov and Oleg Kharkhardin of the CPSU International Department.

The host for this meeting was Congressman John Conyers. Others on the committee included the following Democratic Congressmen:

John Burton (CA)	Don Edwards (CA)
Charles Rangel (NY)	Ted Weiss (NY)

Ron Dellums (CA)(4)

In 1982 the House Intelligence Committee released a report on hearings about Soviet Active Measures, including a 48 page WPC document describing the 1978 meeting. But in publishing this report, Democratic Congressman Edward Boland's staff carried out a deliberate cover-up by deleting 14 pages from the WPC document that described the Washington meeting and named the above six Democratic Congressmen involved.

The previous year another WPC delegation had arrived in Washington to promote the Nuclear Freeze campaign. This group was welcomed to the Capitol by a group of Democratic Congressmen including:

John Conyers	Don Edwards
Mervyn Dymally	Mickey Leland
George Crockett	Ted Weiss

These Democratic Congressmen made House offices available for meetings with the WPC delegates.

During one of the meetings in these Congressmen's offices an official of the U.S. Communist Party was present and made a speech recommending that the "peace movement" unite in supporting the cause of several terrorist groups including the PLO and the Communist guerillas in El Salvador.

In 1982 Democratic Congressman Gus Savage of Illinois took part in a parade in Lisbon, Portugal, demonstrating against the policies of NATO. He engaged in this event in spite of clear evidence of Communist backing. Even the Portuguese Socialist Party had boycotted the parade, saying it was " a reflection of the diplomatic and military logic of the Soviet bloc." The Portuguese government had expelled two Soviet KGB officers for being involved in its planning stages.

Savage defended his participation because he was an official of the World Peace Council, which he said is "the largest non-governmental peace organization in the world." (5)

The U.S. Peace Council (USPC).

This organization is the American branch of the World Peace Council. It was founded in 1979 largely by the initiative of the U.S. Communist Party. Michael Myerson, a high ranking CPUSA official, became the Executive Director of the USPC, and Alexandra (Sandy) Pollack, another top CPUSA official, became the USPC's "international solidarity coordinator."

The main purpose of this new organization initially was to promote the cause of the Sandinistas in Nicaragua. The Somoza dictatorship was facing increasing opposition in the country and growing military successes of the Sandinista guerillas. The Carter Administration was pursuing an active policy of undermining Somoza and encouraging the Sandinistas, in spite of evidence that the latter were Communists supported by Castro and the Soviet Union.

Many knowledgeable experts on Central America urged that the U.S. encourage the non-Communist opposition to Somoza and help them to take office. But the left-wingers in the Carter Administration opposed this policy and pushed actions that led to the non-communist democrats being ignored, Somoza fleeing the country, and the Sandinistas seizing power and installing their totalitarian Communist regime.

A major player in these events was the U. S. Peace Council. It organized a National Conference on Nicaragua in 1979, along with several other radical groups, to discuss a strategy to ensure that the Sandinistas took control. Three Congressmen and two Senators lent support to this Conference: Ron Dellums, Tom Harkin, and Walter Fauntroy in the House, and Mark Hatfield and Edward Kennedy in the Senate. (6)

There are three Republican legislators who frequently lend their support to such left-wing causes: the two Senators from Oregon, Mark Hatfield and Bob Packwood, and Congressman Jim Leach from Iowa. But this is hardly comparable to the widespread cooperation with pro-communist causes now found among leaders of the Democratic Party.

A number of other people active in Democratic affairs outside of Congress have been members of the

USPC in spite of its exposure as a Communist front. These include:

Dee Bates of Jesse Jackson's Operation PUSH.

Jack (Hunter Pitts) O'Dell, mentioned earlier as a reported CPUSA official as well as Jesse Jackson's foreign affairs advisor.

Irving Stolberg, prominent member of the Connecticut State Legislature, for several years Speaker of this body.

Mel King, Massachusetts State Representative and former candidate for Mayor of Boston.

Saundra Graham of the Massachusetts legislature.

Gilberto Gerena Valentin, New York City Councilman.

Institute for Policy Studies (IPS).

The Institute for Policy Studies is the largest and most influential of the far left think tanks in Washington. Since its founding in 1964, it has steadily followed a pro-communist line on foreign policy, defense, and the economy, and has spawned a large number of spin-offs, other think tanks and public affairs organizations following the same radical agenda.

Even the liberal *New York Times* ran an article in its magazine section in April 1981 by Joshua Muravchik, describing the Institute's left–wing orientation. (7)

Brian Crozier, former director of the London-based Institute for the Study of Conflict and an authority on propaganda and subversion, wrote that the IPS is "the perfect intellectual front for Soviet activities which would be rejected if they were to originate openly from the KGB."(8)

Known Communists have been officials or staffers of the IPS from time to time, and KGB agents have been seen frequently at their meetings. Among these are:

<u>Orlando Letelier</u>, the former Chilean Foreign Minister under the pro-communist Allende government. Letelier fled to this country after Allende was overthrown. He joined IPS and became head of its European subsidiary, the Transnational Institute (TNI). He became active in a propaganda campaign against the Chilean government and American anti-Communist policy in general. In 1976 Letelier was killed in his auto by a bomb. The FBI recovered his briefcase intact. Its contents included correspondence and records showing that he had been receiving financial support from the Soviet propaganda apparatus working through East Germany and Cuba.

<u>Isabel Letelier</u>, Orlando's widow, is an IPS Fellow.

<u>Tariq Ali</u>, also active with TNI, the IPS subsidiary. Ali was the editor of a Communist newspaper in England, "The Red Mole," and a member of the 4th International Trotskyite Party in Europe.

<u>Susan Weber</u>, at one time editor of an IPS environmental journal, "The Elements." Before joining IPS Ms.Weber worked for the Soviet Embassy as editor of their magazine, "Soviet Life," and was registered with the Justice Department as an employee of a "foreign power."

Roberta Salper, IPS fellow, a member of the Central Committee of the Puerto Rican Socialist Party, a Communist organization.

In 1987 an exhaustive study of IPS was published, written by S. Steven Powell, entitled "Covert Cadre." Powell had worked on this book as a PhD project for six years and had been able to attend many IPS seminars and other meetings and interview IPS personnel. As a student he was given much leeway to attend and even photograph these proceedings.

His book is a graphic expose of the extent of Soviet influence on the IPS and in turn on a large number of members of Congress and their staffs. Powell actually got pictures of at least nine KGB agents and other Soviet personnel from the Soviet Embassy attending IPS affairs and conversing with IPS people. (9)

In spite of its obvious pro-communist orientation, a number of leading Democrats have cooperated closely with the IPS, and have been greatly influenced by it. A few major examples:

– Two of the founders of IPS, Marcus Raskin and Arthur Waskow, had previously worked for Democratic Congressman Robert Kastenmeier of Wisconsin. In 1961 they co-authored a report for him that recommended unilateral disarmament for the U.S.

Kastenmeier is still in the House, with one of the longest records of service (since 1959), and is a member of two committees, Intelligence and Judiciary. The Intelligence Committee is directly concerned with the affairs of the CIA and other American intelligence operations. On the Judiciary Committee Kastenmeier is a member of the

Subcommittee on Civil and Constitutional Rights, and Chairman of the Subcommittee on Courts, Civil Liberties, and the Administration of Justice, both of which have considerable authority over FBI affairs.

The fact that Kastenmeier, who has so much influence on American intelligence operations, has such close ties with two IPS founders, should be a cause of concern.

– In 1975 a group of 47 members of Congress, led by John Conyers, asked the IPS to prepare an "alternative budget" to that proposed by President Ford. This request was repeated in 1976 and 1978, by 56 legislators. The 1978 document called for "a socialist housing program. . .radical social change in the educational system...a 50% cut in the Defense budget". . .and "disengagement" from America's overseas commitments.

In 1983 sixty Congressmen went back to the IPS with a request for another "alternative" budget, showing that this large a number of our legislators are sympathetic to such a radical agenda.

– Congressman George Miller (CA) for many years had an IPS associate fellow, Cynthia Aronson, as his legislative aide doing most of the leg-work and research on Latin American policy.

– Don Edwards, chairman of the Subcommittee on Civil and Constitutional Rights, which has some oversight responsibility over the FBI, was a member of the committee organizing the celebration for IPS's Twentieth Anniversary in 1984. He is married to Edith Wilkie, who has been active for years with various IPS affiliates.

– Congressman Ted Weiss attended a meeting at New York's Riverside Church organized by the

Church's Disarmament Program directed by Cora Weiss (no kin), who works closely with IPS. At this meeting Ted Weiss said "I spend more time at (IPS) than almost any other institution....You provide leadership and substance to people throughout the District."

– Democratic Senator Tom Harkin also supports IPS. At an IPS reception in 1984 he said, "I want to thank the Institute for Policy Studies and the people who worked so hard....and have been in my office a lot."

– Senator John Kerry hired a former IPS fellow, Gareth Porter, to be his legislative aide. Porter is a self-styled expert on Southeast Asia, notable for being one of those defending the bloody Pol Pot regime in Cambodia long after the evidence of its genocide of its own people had become overwhelming. (10)

– Paul Warnke, one of the leading Arms Control experts under Democratic administrations, is closely linked with IPS. He is on the IPS board, has taught at the IPS educational organization, The Washington School, and was the toastmaster at the IPS Twentieth Anniversary celebration.

– The Washington School, founded by IPS in 1978, has been an important institution for influencing Congress and the Democratic Party. Courses on defense, foreign affairs, and domestic policies are taught there by IPS officers and staffers, and other American or foreign radical "experts." A large number of members of Congress and staffers have

attended these schools. Several legislators have also
taught there, including the following:

Tom Harkin	James Abourezk
Paul Tsongas	George Miller
Mark Hatfield	J. William Fulbright
John Conyers	Henry Reuss
Ron Dellums	

Several Democrats who have held important
government positions have also taught at this school
including:

Paul Warnke, former Salt II negotiator and director of the Arms Control and Disarmament Agency
under Carter.

Morton Halperin, former Deputy Assistant
Secretary of Defense and member of the National
Security Council.

W. Anthony Lake, Director of the State
Department Policy Planning Staff under Carter.

Dr. Powell points out in "Covert Cadre" that
when these prominent Democrats lecture at IPS
Washington School courses, the "students" often
include a number of radicals who will ask leading
questions. By this technique they are in effect edu-
cating the lecturers according to the "Socratic
Method."

Thus IPS has been another conduit for the
Soviets and their Communist proxies to influence
the liberal wing of the Democratic Party.

National Lawyers Guild (NLG)

This important legal front was founded in
1936 by an earlier Communist front called the
International Labor Defense, which was the U.S. sec-
tion of the Soviet-controlled International Red Aid.
In 1946 the NLG became affiliated with the
International Association of Democratic Lawyers
(IADL), the new international Communist front for
attorneys.

Today the NLG has several thousand members,
offices in 50 cities, units in most of the leading law
schools, and a major operation in Washington. It was
cited several times as a Communist front in House
and Senate Internal Security Committees' meetings.
As mentioned earlier, one small but significant indication of the NLG's orientation is that its 1973 convention in Austin, Texas, concluded with a singing of
the Communist anthem, "The Internationale":

> **"Tis the final conflict. Let each
> stand in his place. The International
> Soviet shall be the human race!"**

Among the NLG officers have been such radicals as:

Victor Rabinowitz, who took the Fifth
Amendment on four occasions before Congressional
committees when asked about membership in the
Communist Party.

Bernadine Dohrn, member of the violent
Weather Underground, and until recently in hiding
as a fugitive from justice.

Doris Walker, member of the law firm Treuhoff, Walker and Bernstein. Treuhoff is an admitted Communist, married to Jessica Mitford, another admitted Communist.

Jonathan Lubell, identified as a Communist while at Harvard Law School.

William Kunstler, the radical lawyer. Kunstler made a speech at the NLG Convention in Colorado in 1971, concluding with the cry, "I am a double agent. I am using the System to bring down the System." This statement speaks for itself.

In spite of these Communist origins and activities, the NLG has gained the cooperation of many leading Democrats. As mentioned earlier, Senator Metzenbaum was Secretary at one time. Congressman George Crockett was once a Vice President. Many others who wield considerable influence on the policies of leading Democratic officials have been associated with the Guild. These include:

Robert Borosage, president of IPS, formerly head of the Guild's Washington office.

Morton Halperin, now head of the Center for National Security Studies, cited above as consistently opposing a strong U.S. intelligence effort and ignoring Soviet espionage and subversion. Formerly Chairperson of the Campaign to Stop Government Spying, which was launched at a large conference in 1977 organized by the NLG.

SANE/Freeze

SANE, or the Committee for a Sane Nuclear Policy, was originally an organization of sincere liberals concerned about nuclear proliferation. But it became increasingly radical after David Cortright took over as Director. Cortright earned a "PhD" by a course of study at IPS, although IPS is not accredited to give such degrees. He was active with another IPS spin-off, the Center for National Security Studies, which is dedicated to attacking U.S. intelligence organizations but has never issued any reports on the threat of Communist intelligence operating against the U.S.

SANE later merged with the Freeze campaign office after the latter's effort to get a nuclear "freeze" passed by Congress had failed. Another Director of the combined organization is the Rev. William Sloane Coffin, the radical clergyman who left New York's Riverside Church after he and Cora Weiss with their "Disarmament Program" had almost brought that large church into bankruptcy.

SANE/Freeze has considerable influence among Congressional liberals. Dr. Powell conducted a telephone survey and found that 78% of House liberals' offices read SANE material and 54% of the Senate offices.

SANE was a major participant in the events welcoming the WPC delegations to Capitol Hill described above. On May 31, 1981, Representatives John Conyers, Ron Dellums, and Patricia Schroeder invited their fellow Congressmen and staffs to attend a SANE-sponsored briefing on "European Opposition to the New Generation of Nuclear Weapons." Speakers were Richard Barnet of IPS and an Italian Communist, Nino Pasti, former NATO general and now a WPC member. This was timed to coincide with the Soviet campaign against the introduction of U.S. Pershings and Cruise Missiles in Western Europe, which eventually were successfully installed to offset the serious Soviet advantage in short range missiles.

Staffers of the following Democratic Congressmen involved with arms control issues also told Dr. Powell that they found SANE materials valuable:

Berkeley Bedell (IA)
Barbara Boxer (CA)
Bob Carr(MI).

CISPES

The Committee in Solidarity with the People of El Salvador (CISPES) is another Communist front receiving substantial backing from prominent Democrats.

In 1982 the Salvadoran Army discovered a Communist guerilla safe house and found several documents including a report by a Communist agent, Farid Handal, describing his trip to the U.S. to set up a propaganda network. Farid Handal is the brother of the head of the Salvadoran Communist party, Shafik Handal. He traveled to the U.S. in 1980 and visited several major cities. He had the cooperation of the Cuban UN Mission and the CPUSA and especially Sandy Pollack, as well as the U.S. Peace Council.

Pollack organized for him a national conference of representatives from the USPC, some radical trade union people, IPS, and other front groups to establish a support mechanism for a solidarity committee. The Communist Party put him in touch with Congressman Ron Dellums. Dellums made office space available and arranged a meeting for Handal with the Congressional Black Caucus.

Handal wrote in his report:

> **"Monday morning the offices of Congressman Ron Dellums were turned into our offices. Everything was done there. The meeting with the Black Caucus took place in the liver of the monster itself, nothing less than the meeting room of the House Foreign Affairs Committee." (11)**

CISPES now has offices or affiliates in more than 300 cities and university campuses around the country. It refuses to name its board of directors, claiming to be only a grass roots citizens organization. It has consistently backed the cause of the Communist guerillas. It opposed even humanitarian aid to the Duarte government, the first democratically-elected regime in Saldvadoran history.

Although CISPES' Communist origins were widely publicized in State Department and other official documents, it has received the support of several prominent Democrats. (Official reports containing information on CISPES Communist origins include: "Soviet Active Measures," Hearings Before the House Intelligence Committee, July 13 & 14, 1982, p. 45; "News Briefings on Intelligence Information on External Support of the Communist Guerillas in El Salvador," Department of State and Department of Defense, July 18, 1984.) In addition to Ron Dellums it has also had fund-raising letters signed by Representatives Mervyn Dymally and Pat Schroeder. Other Democratic Congressmen giving CISPES support include:

Walter Fauntroy (DC)	James Oberstar (MN)
Robert Toricelli (NY)	James Weaver (OR)
Ted Weiss (NY)	

In 1985 a CISPES lobbying effort persuaded the House Western Hemisphere Affairs Sub-committee under Democrat Michael Barnes to hold a hearing on the "air war" in El Salvador. The object was to attempt to demonstrate that strikes against the guerillas by the Salvadoran air force were in fact strikes against Salvadoran civilians, in violation of Congressional conditions for aid. The leading witness was Gus Newport, Vice Chairman of the World Peace Council and pro-communist mayor of Berkeley (Dellums' home district). This accusation was also made in a written report by Carlotta Scott, Ron Dellums' chief aide. (12)

Thus CISPES is another major conduit by which the Communists have manipulated many prominent Democrats to advance Communist goals. In this case the goal is to promote the victory of the terrorist Communist guerillas in El Salvador by attacking a hard-pressed government elected with a voter turn-out of more than 80% in spite of violent guerilla attempts at disruption.

Coalition for a New Foreign and Military Policy (CNFMP).

This Coalition was founded in 1976 in a merger of other left–wing action groups with major assistance from the radical Institute for Policy Studies. It grew to include representatives of more than 40 organizations including left–wing labor, civic, "peace" and public interest groups and delegates from the Washington offices of many mainline religious denominations.

Its headquarters were first located at 120 Maryland Avenue. This is one of two adjacent town houses owned by Stewart Mott, the GM heir and major supporter of many left–wing causes. Mott's buildings also housed such front groups as Women

Strike for Peace, the Center for Defense Information
and the Center for National Security Studies, which
regularly attack U.S. foreign and defense
policies.(13)

This Coalition has had the support of a large
number of Senators and Congressmen and in turn
has had major influence in lobbying Congress against
a strong defense policy and resistance to
Communism in Central America and elsewhere.
Some major examples:

Democratic Senator <u>Tom Harkin</u> has worked
closely with the Coalition and IPS in attacking U.S.
foreign policy. While still a Congressman, Harkin introduced an amendment to the Foreign Assistance
Act in 1975 to tie assistance to a nebulous standard
of human rights. George McGovern sponsored this
amendment in the Senate. While it sounds fair, the
amendment in practice has been used by radicals in
Congress frequently to deny aid to governments hard
pressed in their struggles against Communist guerillas.

Cynthia Aronson of IPS was a leader of the
Coalition's strategy on this measure. Harkin and
McGovern later wrote the Coalition a letter thanking
them for being a major influence in getting passage.

<u>Former Senator James Abourezk</u>, a trustee of
IPS, also worked closely with the Coalition.

In 1978 the Coalition called a press conference for Harkin announcing that he would work for
drastic cuts in arms sales to countries run by dictators—Iran, Indonesia, the Philippines, and Nicaragua.
The following year the governments of Iran and
Nicaragua fell to pro-communist forces.

The Coalition takes credit for stopping the Anti-Ballistic Missile program and a halt in the B-1 bomber plans. An analysis by Steven Powell reported in his book, "Covert Cadre" shows that in 1983 79 Congressmen voted the straight Coalition line. All but one (Jim Leach) were Democrats. Eighteen Senators did the same, including presidential candidate Gary Hart, six out of the eight Democratic members of the Foreign Relations Committee, and the Chairman of the Appropriations Committee. These legislators supported the nuclear freeze, opposed covert operations in Nicaragua, chemical weapons, the MX missile, anti-satellite weapons, the B-1 bomber, and the Cruise and Pershing missiles.(14)

The Coalition closed down in 1989 but its operations on Central America have been continued by a "Central American Working Group" located in the Coalition's former offices in Washington. This group continues to work against the U.S. policy of aiding the anti-communist forces in Central America. This is shocking!

Organizations Operating Within Congress.

While the above section described front groups with which prominent Democrats have cooperated, the following section describes two organizations operating within Congress itself made up entirely of legislators and their staffers.

The Arms Control and Foreign Policy Caucus (ACFPC).

This is ostensibly a non-partisan organization on which both Democrats and Republicans serve. But in practice it has been strongly influenced by the most radical of the Democrats and has followed a consistent line against U.S. policy opposing Communism around the world.

The Caucus was founded in 1966, and was originally called Members of Congress for Peace Through Law. From the beginning it has had close ties to the radical Institute for Policy Studies. Five of its founders participated in a 1966 IPS seminar entitled "New Era of American Foreign Policy and Statecraft." Of these, three are still in Congress:

John Conyers
Don Edwards
Robert Kastenmeier

Another one of the five, Philip Burton, died in 1985, but his wife, Sala Burton, replaced him in Congress and on the Caucus. The fifth member, Donald Fraser, was later defeated for Congress but became Mayor of Minneapolis. There, he was notable for having hosted a Soviet delegation attending a 1983 IPS "disarmament" conference.

By 1985 the Caucus membership included 120 Representatives and 15 Senators. Congressman George Miller (CA), chairman of the Caucus' important Latin American Task Force has as his aide Cynthia Aronson, an IPS Associate Fellow. The ultraliberal Republican Senator, Mark Hatfield, is now Chairman of the Caucus. Hatfield, as outlined earlier on page 73, also has close ties to the IPS.

Executive Director of the Caucus is Edith B. Wilkie. Wilkie is also affiliated with IPS. She is active with the Coalition for a New Foreign and Military Policy and is married to Congressman Don Edwards. Edwards is Chairman of the influential Subcommittee on Civil and Constitutional Rights and is another supporter of IPS, having been on the IPS 20th Anniversary Committee.

Following are figures showing the proportion of legislators on key committees belonging to the Caucus:

Democratic members of the House Foreign Affairs Committee – 14 out of 23.

Subcommittee on Human Rights and International Organizations – 6 out of 9.

Subcommittee on Western Hemisphere Affairs (which has responsibility for Central America) – 6 (all Democrats) out of 10. (15)

Typical of its work is a report prepared by the Caucus staff and published by the CNFMP in February 1985 entitled "U.S. Aid to El Salvador: An Evaluation of the Past, A Proposal for the Future." This stated that "the administration has provided insufficient, misleading, and in some cases false information to Congress." It recommended stopping all U.S. funding for the "air war" and said the U.S. must "unequivocally reject a military solution." (16)

The Caucus has opposed almost every new weapons system. (17) Thus, through the indirect influence of the IPS and other fronts, Communist propaganda has continued to succeed in influencing U.S. policy, especially through ultra-liberal members of Congress, mainly the Democrats.

Congressional Black Caucus

It is true that Blacks have experienced a long history of discrimination, one example of which I witnessed during my job in the War Production Board in Washington in World War II, as described earlier. Although this history is gradually coming to an end, we can still give them sympathy for wanting to organize their own cooperative group. But the fact remains that the Congressional Black Caucus, to which all Blacks in Congress belong, has been taken over almost entirely by the radicals.

This is exactly in line with Communist Party objectives. CPUSA publications are full of references to the need to infiltrate the Democratic Party through the Black community. On June 9, 1983, writing in *The Daily World*, Charlene Mitchell, Executive Director of the CPUSA's Afro-American Commission, wrote:

> "To date, most of the debate has centered on the personalities of potential Black candidates and the pros and cons of such a challenge. The thrust of such a candidacy must be to develop the popular electoral base to prevent the Democratic Party from continuing its shift to the right and force a more <u>progressive platform and program in the 1984 campaign</u>.

> "While such a candidacy is explicitly within the <u>Democratic Party</u>, it would objectively signal a high point in the fight for <u>political independence</u>."

This is a clear description of the Communists' strategy of using Blacks to manipulate the Democratic Party and of their objective of promoting "independence" within the Party (i.e., a breaking away of major groups that will cooperate more closely with Communist objectives.)

Political Affairs for March 1989 gives a further description of this strategy:

"We (Communists) see building political <u>independence</u> based on the alliance of Labor with the African-American community as the aim for changing the relationship of forces in elected office. The Party Program maintains that the ultimate expression of this would be a mass <u>anti-monopoly people's party</u>.

"This fact poses sharp questions which center around what role, if any, should the Communist Party play in relation to the main line of development of the empowerment movement forces which for now and the foreseeable future have chosen to wage their struggle mainly within the framework of the Democratic Party.

"Should the Party strive to play a leading role helping these forces gain and consolidate new positions of strength even <u>inside the Democratic Party</u>, or shouldn't it? <u>I think it should.</u>

"This, in my opinion, cannot and should not repose solely on Communist or Left independent candidates. Not if there is any intention of <u>emerging</u> as an integral component of the <u>overall progressive coalition</u>, especially in view of the fact that the Jackson-led <u>progressive wing</u> of the <u>Democratic Party</u> is that coalition's major organized component." (Emphasis added.) (17)

The same issue of *Political Affairs* contained another clear statement of this strategy, which was quoted earlier but is worth repeating:

> "Organized mass movements – especially the African American community, the Rainbow Coalition, labor on all levels, SANE-Freeze, and other mass organizations – become more <u>independent</u> of the Democratic Party establishment on policy and in political direction, but more <u>organizationally involved</u> in the Democratic Party."

This is the clearest statement to date of the strategy of manipulating the Democratic Party to promote "the forces of independence," i.e., forces which can operate within the Democratic structure and yet be independent of traditional Democratic principles and free to promote Communist objectives.

Another example from the same issue of *Political Affairs*:

> "This much is clear – the overall movement will grow. So will the role of the Rainbow Coalition and the labor movement. And it will unfold in the 1989-92 quadrennial cycle <u>primarily</u> but not exclusively, through the medium of the <u>Democratic Party</u>."

In promoting their strategy of using the Black community as one avenue to manipulate the Democratic Party, the Communists have, of course, paid primary attention to Black politicians, in particular those elected to Congress, who can influence national policy. The effort thus has come to a special concentration point with the Congressional

Black Caucus. In May 1987 *Political Affairs* wrote as follows:

> "The role of the Congressional Black Caucus, the most active and <u>progressive</u> bloc in Congress, illustrates the level of sophistication the Afro-American people have reached in utilizing the legislative power."

Ronald Dellums and other radical Black politicians made a concerted effort as soon as they reached Washington to move Blacks in Congress to the Left. Their primary vehicle was the Congressional Black Caucus.

This strategy is cited by Peter Collier and David Horowitz, who knew Dellums in the early days when they were all young radicals in California. Collier and Horowitz were editors of the left–wing *Ramparts* magazine. They later became disillusioned with the radical movement and wrote a dramatic book, "Destructive Generation," a history of the inner workings of the extreme Left. In this they describe how Dellums rose out of the Movement in Berkeley, California, but then began to moderate his radical rhetoric to avoid alienating the voters. "Congressman Dellums," they write, "needed to keep the peace among fractious radicals at home so he could devote his attention to Washington, where he was part of a small group trying to steer the Congressional Black Caucus toward an ultra-left identity." (18)

The Communist *Daily World* on October 4, 1986, reported favorably on a CBC three-day conference in Washington at which plans for electing CBC candidates to Congress were discussed.

The Caucus has in fact followed a consistently Far Left line, opposing all new weapons systems and Administration efforts to assist anti-communist forces abroad. Dellums' position on the Armed Services Committee and Chairman of its Subcommittee on Military Installations and Facilities gives him access to quantities of classified information and great influence on foreign and military policy.

Congressman George Crockett, another CBC leader, has similar access to classified information and influence on Central American policy as Chairman of the Subcommittee on Western Hemisphere Affairs.

Among the most glaring examples of such biassed actions are the following:

Ron Dellums and other members of the CBC cooperated closely with the Salvadoran Communist agent, Farid Handal, on his trip to the U.S. in 1980 to set up a "solidarity" network as a front to promote support for the Salvadoran Communist guerillas. As described in more detail above on page 51, Dellums worked with the CPUSA official, Sandy Pollack, in promoting Handal's efforts, made office space available to him and arranged a meeting for this Communist agent with the entire Black Caucus in the House Foreign Affairs Committee hearing room.

Handal's efforts led to the formation of the Committee in Solidarity with the People of El Salvador, CISPES, which now has branches in 300 cities and university campuses. CBC members have been closely affiliated with CISPES ever since. The Caucus gave early support to the pro-communist regime in Grenada. In 1980 the Carter Administration rejected the appointment of one Dessima Williams to be Grenadan Ambassador to the

U.S. The State Department disapproved the appointment because Miss Williams had been involved in a gun-smuggling ring out of Washington.

Congressman Mervyn Dymally, Chairman of the CBC's Task Force on the Caribbean, had a meeting with Maurice Bishop, Grenadan Prime Minister and head of the pro-communist New Jewel Movement. When the Reagan Administration took office in 1981, the CBC sent a letter to Alexander Haig, the new Secretary of State, supporting Miss Williams' appointment as ambassador, saying that "We can assure you that Grenada wants friendly and close ties with the United States....The Congressional Black Caucus stands ready to facilitate a meeting (between the two governments)."(19)

The Bishop regime, with Cuban and Soviet help, had started construction of a major airfield at Point Salines, Grenada. They claimed that this was for civilian traffic only, but two factors made it obvious that it was for Soviet strategic purposes: the large size of the runways and the presence of Soviet Ambassador Sazhenev, formerly a four star General in the Soviet strategic bomber forces. (20)

In 1982 Dellums and some CBC staffers travelled to Grenada to "investigate" the airport. Their final report to Congress concluded that "nothing being done in Grenada constitutes a threat to the United States or her allies."

Documents later found in Grenada after the U.S. liberation mission revealed that Dellums had actually sent the first draft of this report to Bishop for approval. The documents further revealed that one of Dellums' chief aides on the trip, Carlotta Scott, had a romantic relationship with Bishop. A letter written on Congressional stationery said, "I still love you madly....Ron (Dellums) has become truly committed to Grenada....and just has to get all his thoughts in order as to how your interests can best be served."

Even after a Communist faction under Hudson Austin staged a coup against the Bishop regime and murdered Bishop himself, the CBC continued to support the Grenadan Communist government. They attacked the Reagan Administration's mission to liberate the island in cooperation with other Caribbean governments.

Dessima Williams stayed in the U.S. and continued to stir up opposition to U.S. policy with CBC support for more than a year after her diplomatic visa was revoked. She was arrested by the INS and spent a night in jail. At her hearing, she received assistance from an aide to Congressman Mickey Leland of the CBC. (21)

On January 10, 1990, two leading members of the Caucus, Ron Dellums and George Crockett, joined with 67 other radicals in a full page ad in *The New York Times*. This was an open letter to President Bush attacking his Panama policy. The ad said the "invasion of Panama is illegal" and "We object to the idea that we can impose democracy on another nation." The CBC members and other ad signatories ignored the fact that polls show that the vast majority of the Panamanian and American people support the Administration's policy.

Another indication of the CBC's anti-defense and pro-communist bias is provided by the ratings released by the American Security Council. This private non-profit Council, which is dedicated to supporting a strong U.S. defense, rates all Congressmen and Senators annually based on their voting record on ten major defense and foreign affairs issues during the previous year.

The ratings range from 0% to 100%, depending on the percent of the 10 major issues on which the legislator voted favorably. For the 1987-88 period the ratings for the following leading CBC members were 0% in every case except for Savage, Espy, and Hawkins, who rated 10%.

Ron Dellums	Gus Savage
Bill Gray	Floyd Flake
John Conyers	Augustus Hawkins
Mickey Leland	George Crockett
Charles Rangel	Mike Espy
Marvyn Dymally	Alan Dixon
John Lewis (22)	

Thus the Congressional Black Caucus is another major example of the Communists and their non-communist helpers manipulating the Democratic Party by using conduits through the Black community.

NOTES

1. Bill Gertz, "Soviet Failure to Cut UN Mission Prompted U.S. Drive Against Spies," *Washington Times*, November 3, 1986.
2. (e.g.) "Soviet Active Measures: The World Peace Council," Foreign Affairs Notes, State Department, April 1985.
3. David Martin and John Rees, "Soviet Deception in the United States," in *Mesmerized by the Bear*, edited by Dr. Raymond S. Sleeper, Dodd Mead & Co.
4. *The Mindzsenty Report*, St. Louis, Mo., January 1988, p.1.
5. Ibid. p.2.
6. *Daily World*, February 8, 1979, quoted in L. Francis Bouchey, J. Michael Waller, and Steve Baldwin, "The Real Secret War," Council for Inter-American Security, Washington, D.C, 1987, p. 138.
7. Joshua Muravchik, "The Think Tank on the Left," *The Compact N.Y.Times Magazine*, April 1981, p. 124.
8. Quoted in Brownfeld p.16.
9. S. Steven Powell, *Covert Cadre*, Green Hill, Ottawa, Ill. 1987, photographs following page 163.
10. Porter's testimony defending Pol Pot before a Congressional committee as late as 1977 is quoted in James L. Tyson, *Target America*, Regnery Gateway, Chicago, 1981, p. 128.
11. Quoted in Peter Collier and David Horowitz, *Destructive Generation*, Summit Books, New York, 1989, p. 158. 12. Collier and Horowitz, p. 160.
13. Information on the Coalition's founding is summarized in James L. Tyson, *Prophets or Useful Idiots?*, Council for the Defense of Freedom, Washington, 1988, p. 52.
14. Powell, Appendices 12 and 13, p.386-9. 15. Powell, p. 258.

15. This report was signed by Democratic Congressman George Miller and by two ultra-liberal Republicans, Jim Leach and Mark Hatfield, but as mentioned earlier, the large majority of the Caucus members are Democrats and the Staff reflects this.
16. "Members of Congress for Peace Through Law," Heritage Foundation Institute Analysis, 1977, p.1.
17. *Political Affairs*, March 1989, p.30.
18. Collier & Horowitz, p. 196.
19. Allan C. Brownfeld & J. Michael Waller, *The Revolution Lobby*, p. 68.
20. Ibid. p. 71.
21. Ibid. p. 73.
22. *Human Events*, September 2, 1989, p.10.

Chapter 5

The Effects of this Communist Campaign on Democratic Policy

These Communist efforts have been a major cause of a massive shift to the Left by the Democratic Party in recent years. This has been especially serious in Foreign Affairs and Defense, and in particular on policy against Communism and the Soviets' objectives for promoting Communism around the world.

The move to the Left of the Democratic leadership becomes more obvious if we compare it to the earlier history of the party, which had a great record of opposing tyranny, whether Fascist or Communist.

For years after World War II, the Democratic Party and its leaders were notable for a number of innovative and effective policies to resist Communism. In the late 1940s, when it became obvious that the USSR was not interested in a stable peace but was continuing Lenin's policy of promoting world Communism, the Truman Administration began a series of major actions including:

– The revival of the Voice of America, plus a Russian service for the first time.

– Formation of the CIA.

– The Marshall Plan, to assist Western Europe recover from war devastation and resist Communist subversion.

– The Truman Doctrine, which declared that the U.S. would support any country facing Communist aggression. This was first invoked in order to get a grant of $400 million to assist Greece and Turkey.

– Launching of Radio Free Europe and Radio Liberty to broadcast to Eastern Europe and the Soviet Union with programs addressed to the interests of their own people.

– Covert aid to help defeat the Communist Parties in elections in France and Italy.

– NATO, the major cooperative effort for Western European defense. This was the first mutual defense treaty in American history to involve the stationing of our troops on the continent of Europe in peacetime.

These programs were instituted and carried out by a number of Democratic leaders who had no illusions about the threat of Communism, including Harry Truman, Senator Paul Douglas, Henry (Scoop) Jackson, Karl Mundt, William Benton, and Will Clayton (the Assistant Secretary of State for Economic Affairs, who was the real Father of the "Marshall Plan").

This realistic attitude by Democratic leaders continued down through the Kennedy Administration. There were a few major lapses including a fuzzy policy on China, which allowed the brutal Mao Tse Tung regime to take over that huge country, and failure to adequately support the Cuban invasion after Kennedy took office in 1961, allowing

Castro to consolidate power. (These lapses themselves can be at least partly blamed on Communist propaganda and subversion.) Generally, the party was following an enlightened anti-communist line.

The picture began to change gradually but steadily from the Johnson Administration onwards. Johnson himself was anti-communist and attempted to continue the support of the South Vietnamese. He complained often about the growing power of the ultra-liberals, the people who criticized him simply because he hadn't gone to Harvard (like the Kennedys). He also expressed alarm specifically to his subordinates about growing Communist influence on the media and on some members of his party.

Richard Goodwin, one of Johnson's White House assistants, says in his book, "Remembering America," that "Johnson began to hint privately...that he was the target of a gigantic Communist conspiracy in which his domestic advisers were only players, not conscious participants, perhaps, but unwitting dupes."

Goodwin goes on to say that Johnson said "You'd be surprised at how much (the FBI) knows about people. . .This country is in a little more danger than we think. And some one has to uncover this information." (1)

Goodwin adds that he and Bill Moyers, another presidential assistant, became concerned that Johnson was developing symptoms of "paranoid disintegration." They each consulted psychiatrists in confidence. In the light of later developments, however, it seems more likely that Johnson was accurate rather than paranoid.

The Democrats continued to maintain control of both Houses of Congress, but the Democratic majority began to become more and more left-wing as the dissension over Viet Nam (stimulated to a great extent by Communist propaganda) divided the country.

In November 1974 as a result of the shocks of Watergate and growing controversy over Viet Nam, the Democrats won 290 House seats and increased their strength in the Senate from 55 to 66. The new legislators arriving in Washington, "The Viet Nam Generation," gave further impetus to the leftward trend of the Party.

In the 1976 election the Democrats maintained this 2-1 margin in Congress and added control of the White House with the Carter/Mondale ticket. Walter Mondale was a former follower of George McGovern. He and his associates, soon dubbed "The Mondale Mafia," were given several influential posts in the new administration, many in positions involving defense and foreign policy. They had more influence than any former Vice President's entourage in swinging administration policy to the left.

This steady massive move leftward by the Democratic National leadership has continued down to the present.

Republican Congressman Robert Dornan, who was out of office from 1983 to '85, says he was astonished at the further shift to the left of the Democrats in Congress after just two years. "What used to be the extreme left among the Democrats has now become Mainstream," he says. "Bella Abzug used to be considered an extremist Democrat. If she were in the House today, she might be the Majority Leader."

Illinois Republican Henry Hyde says "Marxist thought now enjoys respectability on Capitol Hill."

The leadership, which used to be in the hands of men like Harry Truman, Scoop Jackson, Karl

Mundt, and Jack Kennedy, is now being heavily in-
fluenced by the heirs of George McGovern: Mondale,
Dukakis, Teddy Kennedy, and Jesse Jackson. The
Chairman of the Democratic National Committee is
Jackson's former campaign aide, Ronald Brown.

Rather than resisting Communism, the
Democratic majority is building up a record of coop-
erating with it, or of opposing any efforts to resist
Communist designs.

Less than a year after the Viet Nam disaster,
the Ford Administration was assisting the anti-communist forces in Angola in their struggle against a
Soviet-backed Communist regime for control of the
country after the Portuguese withdrawal. But the
Democrats in Congress passed the so-called Clark
Amendment over Ford's veto, forbidding any such aid
to the anti-communist forces.

This new Democratic attitude was in stark
contrast to President Kennedy's stirring words in his
1961 inaugural address: "We will pay any price, bear
any burden, meet any hardship" to defend freedom
around the world.

One example of the effects of this leftward
swing by the Democrats was the impact on American
broadcasting efforts, which had been initiated by the
Democratic administration of Harry Truman. The
Voice of America and Radio Free Europe/Radio
Liberty, which under the Truman, Eisenhower and
Kennedy Administrations had grown into effective
crusaders for freedom, began to suffer severe cen-
soring of any attempts to criticize Communism or
promote Democracy.

They also experienced cutbacks in their budgets because of the actions of the Democratic
Congress and the Carter Administration. As one example, by the time Reagan took office in 1981, the

Soviets were spending more on jamming our broadcasts than we were on all our broadcasting efforts combined. And the Voice had been so restricted on funds for engineering facilities that it was still using a transmitter in West Germany that had belonged to the Goebbels Propaganda Ministry in Nazi Germany and employed vacuum tube technology.(2)

Another serious effect, which can be directly traced to Communist objectives, has been the virtual destruction of America's internal security, that is, the ability of the Government to monitor subversion and propaganda within this country as carried out by American citizens acting as covert agents of foreign powers.

This is a vital function that used to be shared by a number of important Government organs including the FBI and other branches under the Justice Department, backed up by the investigative powers of the Senate and House.

Such activities, of course, have always been a prime target of the Communists, because they are the main focus of investigations since the defeat of the Nazi and Fascist powers in World War II.

In the 1960s, Communist literature, including the Communist Press, *The Daily World* and *Political Affairs*, announced four major objectives for the Party over the coming years. Abolition of the:

1. House UnAmerican Activities Committee

2. Senate Internal Security Subcommittee

3. The Subversive Activities Control Board

4. The Attorney General's List of Subversive Organizations.

By 1976 <u>all of these objectives had been gained</u>, mainly by the actions of <u>Democratic leaders</u> in Congress. The success of their efforts can be summarized briefly as follows.

The House UnAmerican Activities Committee (HUAC) was the prime target. It had been launched originally before World War II by the Democratically-controlled Congress and with the blessings of the Roosevelt Administration, to investigate the threat of Nazi and Fascist activities in this country, as well as extremist groups like the Ku Klux Klan. It also looked into Communist activities but to a much lesser extent until after World War II.

After 1945 and the growing disillusionment with the true aims of our former ally, the Soviet Union, and growing evidence that they were continuing Communist propaganda and subversion in this country, the House Committee turned increasingly to investigations of Communist activity.

This change of focus began to bring a crowd of critics out of the woodwork who had formerly supported the Committee. In 1957 the Communist Party launched a new front, the National Committee to Abolish HUAC. Later, after the House Committee changed its name to the House Internal Security Committee, the Communist front also changed its own name to the National Committee Against Repressive Legislation (NCARL).

This was directed by two men, Frank Wilkinson and Harvey O'Connor, who had earlier been identified as Communists by witnesses before HUAC hearings.

(Wilkinson had been identified by an under-cover agent of the FBI in 1956. Twice he refused to answer questions about his Party membership before

HUAC. In 1958 he was cited for contempt and later served nine months of a one year jail sentence.) (3)

Such Communist activities against our internal security organs took some years to bear fruit. The Subversive Activities Control Board (SACB) was the first to get the axe, by subtle means. Democratic Senator Proxmire had been trying to kill it for years. In the 1974 budget passed in 1973, the House voted to include it. But in the Senate, Democratic Senator Sam Ervin led an attack, claiming that President Nixon did not have the authority to carry out such activities. Funds for the Board were not approved and it went out of existence.

The Law authorizing the Board is still on the books, however. If and when Congress approves the funds, it could be reinstated.

The House Internal Security Committee was the next to go, killed in the following Congressional session. For many years it had the support of the Republicans and enough Democrats in the House to maintain operations. But by the 1970s with the many shocks of Watergate and Viet Nam, the Communist propaganda began to get results.

In 1974 the Democrats in the House opposed to the Committee forced an up and down vote as to whether or not it should be continued. They lost this vote, since enough Democrats voted with the Republicans to maintain the Committee in operation. But immediately after the House reconvened in January 1975, the Democrats opposed to the Committee managed to maneuver the Democratic Caucus to approve a new set of Rules for the House which omitted the Internal Security Committee.

This was submitted to the entire House. Since these rules also contained a complete set of provisions on the operations of the House, it would have been hard for any Democrats to oppose their leadership by voting against them. So enough stayed loyal and the rules were approved. The Internal Security Committee thus went out of existence, killed by what was only a skillful parliamentary maneuver.

The Senate Internal Security Subcommittee was abolished in a similar subtle fashion four years later. A number of Democratic Senators and the ultra-liberal Republican, Mark Hatfield, had been opposing the Subcommittee for many years. In 1978 they succeeded in creating enough opposition so that it was virtually abolished. But Democratic Senator McClellan, on the Judiciary Committee, with the aid of other sympathetic Senators like Republican Strom Thurmond, managed to get the subcommittee's functions continued under the Criminal Law Subcommittee.

The following year, however, when Teddy Kennedy became Chairman of the Judiciary Committee, he succeeded in abolishing even the Criminal Law Subcommittee. So the functions of the Senate's Internal Security Subcommittee went out of existence for good.

(It was partially revived when the Republicans gained a small majority of the Senate in the 1980 election. A Subcommittee on Security and Terrorism was formed under the Chairmanship of Senator Jeremiah Denton (R–Ala.). But this was so inhibited by its Democratic members and fears of being accused of "McCarthyism" that it never got into the field of internal security. When the Democrats regained control in 1986, this Subcommittee was then killed by Democratic Senator Joe Biden, the new chairman of the Judiciary Committee.)

The Communists along with many ultra-liberal organizations were also waging a steady propaganda campaign against the FBI and its efforts to monitor subversive activities. By 1974 the pressure had grown enormously as a result of the controversies over Viet Nam and a series of Congressional hearings including a special Senate Committee under Democrat Frank Church and a House Committee under Democrat Otis Pike.

The criticisms of FBI abuse of Americans' civil rights became so intense that in 1974 President Ford approved a new series of regulations for the FBI, the so-called "Levi Guidelines" named after his Attorney General, Edward Levi. These ruled that the Bureau could no longer investigate any American citizens or organizations unless there was <u>prior evidence of criminal activity</u>. This took the Bureau entirely out of the business of investigating Americans for propaganda or subversion. (How can you decide if illegal activity is going on until you have investigated?)

The Democratic administration of Franklin D. Roosevelt had been the first to direct the Bureau to investigate American citizens and organizations in order to monitor activities supporting foreign subversion or propaganda. At first this was mainly directed against Nazi and Fascist efforts, but it soon included such other "un-American" activities as the Ku Klux Klan and the Communists.

Up to the time of the Ford Administration the FBI continued this work, but always strictly limited to investigations. It had no power to publicize its results, or to bring people to trial. Indictments for illegal activities could only be brought by the Justice Department based on FBI or other evidence. With the Levi Guidelines, however, even such carefully controlled investigations of subversion virtually ceased. As a result, the number of internal security cases being carried out by the FBI dropped from 24,000 in 1973 to less than 100 by 1978.

The Reagan Administration attempted to restore some of the FBI's ability to monitor Communist subversion. They issued a new set of guidelines that improved the situation only slightly. The Administration was continually hobbled in this effort by the House Subcommittee on Civil and Constitutional Rights, which has an important role in approving FBI policy.

This subcommittee is chaired by Don Edwards, a perennial critic of the FBI. The other Democratic members are Bob Kastenmeier, John Conyers, Pat Schroeder, and Charles Schumer. The first three of these, as well as Don Edwards, appear frequently in this book as representative of the Party's left wing.

ALL OF AMERICA'S INTERNAL SECURITY ORGANIZATIONS HAVE BEEN PUT OUT OF BUSINESS. THERE ARE NO LONGER ANY OFFICIAL BODIES INVESTIGATING COMMUNIST PROPAGANDA AND SUBVERSION CARRIED OUT BY AMERICAN CITIZENS IN THIS COUNTRY. THE U.S. IS VIRTUALLY DEFENSELESS AGAINST SUCH OPERATIONS. THE COMMUNIST OBJECTIVES IN THIS AREA, OUTLINED AS EARLY AS THE 1960S, HAVE ALL BEEN ATTAINED, LARGELY AS THE RESULT OF DEMOCRATIC ACTIONS IN CONGRESS.

In spite of the great news from Eastern Europe and Nicaragua, this propaganda campaign is going on as strongly as ever.

In December 1986 the CPUSA announced another set of "goals." Gus Hall gave a speech before the Central Committee in which he rejoiced over the Communists "victories" in the November election, which restored Democratic control of the Senate. He announced the following four goals for Congress for 1987: 1. End all nuclear testing. 2. Stop Star Wars. 3. Stop all aid to the Contras. 4. Ratify SALT II.

Most of this agenda was in fact implemented during 1987, largely by Congressional action:

– The Iran-Contra investigation resulted in a steep decline in support for the Contras and the departure of many dedicated anti-communists from the Administration. Aid for the Contras was cut drastically.

– The SDI program continued to get funding far below what the Administration requested. Many experts had said that a feasible missile defense could have been launched several years earlier, but with the opposition mainly from Democrats in Congress, the program was limited to research only at a level below that asked by the Administration, and implementation was put off even further into the future.

– Congressional Democrats continued to hold the Administration to a strict interpretation of the SALT II Treaty, although the Senate in fact had never ratified this.

The Communists were jubilant. A headline in *The People's World* for its Christmas Eve issue proclaimed:

"1987 Was A Very Good Year. 1988 Can Be Better."

This *People's World* issue also announced two goals for the Communists in 1988: winning Senate ratification of the INF Treaty and cutting all Contra military aid.

Both goals were soon enacted by the Democratically controlled Congress in 1988. (4)

On many other issues of security and foreign affairs, direct quotes from leading Democrats are further clear signs of this new left-wing bias. On Central

America and the Caribbean, most Democrats have
viewed the problems only as a result of "poverty" or
"oppressive oligarchies" or even Reagan's blundering
militarism. They ignore the influence of the Soviets
and their Cuban proxies. Communist elements are
almost never mentioned, as though the Reagan and
Bush administrations were simply supporting a war
by brutal oligarchical elements against their own
people.

From 1981 through 1989 there was an almost
constant double standard in attacking "violence and
terrorism" by the Contras fighting the Communist
Nicaraguan regime, but in ignoring or attempting to
justify the terrorism of the Salvadorean Communist
guerillas. Likewise, there was a constant barrage of
attacks on the Salvadoran government for being
"dictatorial" and refusing to negotiate with the
Salvadoran Communist guerillas, but a lack of any
demand that the Nicaraguan Government negotiate
with the Contras. A few examples:

After the Grenada liberation operation, which
had the overwhelming support of the Grenadan and
American people, Democratic Congressman Pete
Stark exploded as follows:

> "It is essential, now that the
> President has shown his true colors, that
> the Congress. . .bring this insane Reagan
> foreign policy back into line. . .We are
> rapidly headed down the road not to one
> Vietnam, but possibly two or three, and
> maybe even World War III. Let us stop
> the President before it is too late." (5)

In 1983 Congressman Les AuCoin not only
assaulted the good faith of the democratic forces in
Central America, but at the same time even attacked
the policies of the previous D e m o c r a t i c

administrations of Harry Truman and John Kennedy in opposing Communism, saying:

> "For decades. . .this government, under Democratic and Republican administrations, has been willing to welcome with open arms any government, any tyranny that happens to be clever enough to say the requisite lines. These lines are, 'Hey, I'm anti-communist'. . .My friends, Hitler was anti-communist and no one rushed to give him aid. And I do not think it is in the interests of the United States to be giving aid and comfort to his imitators in Central America."

(How false this statement looks today. Would AuCoin compare Mrs. Chamorro to Hitler, after her victory over the Communist Sandinista regime in Nicaragua?)

Ted Weiss in 1983:

> "Our country's interests in Central America are not based on some real or imagined Soviet threat there. The problem in El Salvador, Nicaragua, and the other nations of Central America are of their own making, deeply based in political and economic history." (6)

In 1984 Democratic Congressman Steve Solarz said:

> "In almost every corner of the globe, four years of Republican foreign policy have made the world a more dangerous place to live. In Central America...its policies are leading us ineluctably towards the introduction of

American combat forces into El Salvador and possibly Nicaragua as well." (How untrue this statement looks today.)

Alan Cranston in 1985:

> "One of my proudest achievements is that I helped get us out of that tragic, sorry war (Viet Nam). Since then, I've helped keep us out of war in Angola. And I've helped prevent a war in Panama. I'm working in the Senate now to keep us out of war in Central America. . .I oppose the <u>terrorists</u> who are trying to overthrow the government of Nicaragua." (e.a.)

(The Nicaraguan Freedom Fighters Cranston calls "terrorists" are not in fact terrorists, but Nicaraguans trying to restore Democracy to their country.)

Gerry Studds in 1986:

> "The Administration has argued that military pressure will produce a negotiated settlement in Nicaragua. But history lends little support to the notion that "low level war" is a prelude to peace...that arming the Contras will bring Democracy to Nicaragua." (7)

(A year after Studds' statement, the Arias Peace Plan was signed leading to heavily monitored elections, in which Democracy was restored to Nicaragua. This was at least partly the results of the pressure from the Nicaraguan Democratic Resistance.)

Pat Schroeder in 1987:

"I think everybody in this
hemisphere feels like they are stuffed in
a bathtub with an elephant, and we are
the elephant, and we just stomp all over
everybody and, you know, it is not a
pleasant place to be."(8)

(Would the people of Panama, recently
liberated from a cruel dictator, or the people of
Nicaragua, who have recently voted overwhelmingly
for Democracy, agree with this idiotic statement?)

On Central America, the Democrats constantly
called on the El Salvadoran government to negotiate
with the Communist guerillas, but never
recommended that the Nicaraguan government
negotiate with the democratic resistance forces
there. Nor did many Democrats support aid to these
Freedom Fighters that would pressure the Sandinista
government into negotiations. The Salvadoran
Communist guerillas, who have been waging a long
term terrorist campaign, involving the assassination
of more than 20 local mayors in the past two years,
are referred to by the Democrats only as "the
opposition." In contrast, the pro-democracy
Freedom Fighters in Nicaragua are generally referred
to as "terrorists." Some examples of these double
standards:

Howard Wolpe in 1982:

"It is ironic that we should, once
again, find ourselves on the side of those
who would try to block change and to
prevent reform....Our government is
making the same tragic mistake in El
Salvador as it has so often before in its
dealings with the developing world—that

of equating political stability with the status quo." (9)

Ted Kennedy in 1983:

"Rather than move toward a peaceful political solution in El Salvador, the Reagan Administration has continued to pursue a policy of military escalation. Rather than work with our friends and allies in the region to resolve the outstanding disputes within and among the nations of Central America, this Administration has paid lip-service to the idea of such cooperation, while attaching unacceptable preconditions to any negotiations." (10)

George Miller in 1984:

"We must deny the Administration the means to pursue a military solution in El Salvador, by cutting military aid. Instead the Reagan Administration and the Salvadoran government must take the necessary steps to find a negotiated solution to the war and to punish those responsible for massive brutality." (11)

Tony Coelho in 1988:

"This Administration is committed for a military victory for the Contras. They don't want peace. They don't want democracy. They want the Contras in charge of Central America because that's what the right wing wants."(12)

(Untrue. Nicaragua now has a democratic administration following an election brought about mainly by pressure from the "Contras.")

This attitude against a strong anti-communist policy in Central America continues right down to the present, in spite of the growing evidence of popular disillusionment with Communism all over the world. The Bush Administration's operation in Panama and seizure of General Noriega was greeted with almost hysterical approval by the Panamanian people and backed almost unanimously by Americans. Yet the Communist Party USA began to attack the move immediately. It released a number of articles claiming that "prisoners are being shot" and atrocity allegations.

Several prominent Democrats immediately began to parallel the CPUSA line in attacking the policy.

Don Edwards called the operation "a trigger-happy act of gunboat diplomacy that continues our mindless 100-year old abuse of small Central American nations."

Ron Dellums said the invasion violated the Constitution and various treaties and added that "Unilateral military intervention in the military affairs of our Latin neighbors has been a consistent first recourse rather than a last resort in our conduct of hemispheric foreign policy."

Robert E. White, Ambassador to El Salvador in the Carter Administration, also attacked the policy. Daniel Ellsberg appeared at a small rally in San Francisco and demanded the impeachment of Bush.(13)

Jesse Jackson appeared on ABC's "Good Morning America" and went so far as to compare the U.S. move to the Tiananmen Square massacre. He made the claims that the U.S. had killed more than 1,200 people and that civilians were buried in "mass graves," sheer undocumented propaganda.

On January 10, 1990, *The New York Times* ran a full-page ad on the back page of the first section, an open letter to President Bush attacking his Panama policy.

The ad said the invasion was "illegal" and violated the Constitution, the OAS charter, and the Canal Treaties. It said Noriega's repression did not "justify interfering with the sovereign nation of Panama." (It did not mention that Noriega himself had destroyed the sovereignty of the <u>Panamanian people</u> and President Bush had <u>restored</u> sovereignty to the people of Panama.)

The ad was signed by 69 people, including:

– Two members of the Congressional Black Caucus:

George Crockett
Ron Dellums

– Six other present or former Democratic legislators or closely associated with Democratic administrations:

James Abourezk
Ramsey Clark
William Fulbright
Henry Gonzales
George McGovern
Robert White, former Ambassador to El
       Salvador

– Thirteen people associated with the National Lawyers Guild or the Institute for Policy Studies or its related front groups:

Richard Barnet
Robert Borosage
The Rev. William Sloane Coffin
Adam Hochschild, President, *Mother Jones*
Saul Landau
Gerald Lefcourt
Victor Rabinowitz
Marcus Raskin
Michael Ratner
Morton Stavis
Cora Rubin Weiss
Peter Weiss
Roger Wilkins.

Such a full-page ad costs $40,000. It was sponsored by "The Ad Hoc Committee for Panama" based in New York City. We can ask what this committee really hopes to accomplish for the Panamanian people, or for the hemispheric war on drugs, which has been greatly advanced by the U.S. move, and we can also ask who paid for this ad?

The ad is another example of "progressive" Democrats and their allies parroting a line parallel to the Communists'.

NOTES

1. Richard N. Goodwin, *Remembering America*, Little Brown & Co., Boston, 1988, p. 402-405.
2. This decline of our broadcasting effort is described in *U.S.International Broadcasting and National Security*, by James L. Tyson, National Strategy Information Center, New York, 1983.
3. These activities and the results of House Committee hearings are summarized in *Protecting Traitors, Spies, and Terrorists*, Church League of America, Wheaton, Ill., 1978, pp.43.44.
4. These events are summarized in John A.Stormer, *None Dare Call It Treason - 25 Years Later*, Liberty Bell Press, Florissant, Mo. 1990.
5. Congressional Record. 10/25/83, pp.E5103-04.
6. CR. 4/28/83 p. H2483.
7. CR. 4/10/86 p. H1769.
8. CR. 6/8/87 p. H4305.
9. CR. 4/20/82 p. E1621.
10. CR. 7/20/83 p. 10521.
11. CR. 2/28/84 p. H949.
12. *Washington Times*, 1/19/88, p.A10.
13. *Information Digest*, 1/12/90, p. 2.

Chapter 6

Conclusions and Recommendations

As the preceding chapters have shown, the Communists have succeeded for many years in infiltrating or otherwise manipulating the liberal wing of the Democratic Party. Under the labels of "Progressive" or "all peoples' forces" or "forces of independence" the many groups appearing to operate independently on their own agendas have in fact been promoting the aims of the Communists, either wittingly or unwittingly.

I believe strongly, as a long time registered Democrat, that this represents a greater threat to our country and our multi-party system than the scandals that have troubled some of our Democratic Party leaders during the past year such as the Oliver North matter. The North matter was <u>trivial</u> compared to this far greater danger to our country and to our democratic form of government. Yet your Congress continues to "push this matter under the rug" hoping no one will discuss it. They are scared of being called "McCarthyites." This is a groundless fear on their part. We have written this book devoid of "McCarthyism" to bring this matter out into the open, and we hope you will also write—to your Senators and Congressman.

As quoted earlier in this book, the Communists have stated frankly in their own publications their aims to work through the Democratic Party. Their magazine, *Political Affairs*, published another clear statement of this strategy in its issue of September/October 1988:

> **"In the absence of a mass-based third party, it is possible and necessary for the people's movement to make use of the <u>Democratic Party</u> in the struggle for reforms. Either that or be shut out of influencing elected office on most levels in the foreseeable future."**

A small well organized minority among Democratic leaders has succeeded in dragging the entire party to the Left in its national and international policies.

The McGovernite wing has virtually taken control of the Party, even though George McGovern himself suffered one of the worst defeats in history in his presidential race against a rather uncharismatic opponent like Richard Nixon in 1972.

McGovern himself wrote in 1988, "I believe that a majority of the American people now accept the views that I advocated in 1972. To repudiate the McGovern Democrats in 1988 is to repudiate what is now the mainstream of the Democratic Party."(1)

The first sentence is nonsense, when we consider the fact that in the 1988 election the American people rejected another McGovernite Democratic candidate, Michael Dukakis, by almost as large a margin as they had spurned McGovern. But the second sentence is absolutely correct. McGovernites like Jackson and Dukakis were able to beat out the more moderate Democratic contenders, or even to discourage many of them like Sam Nunn of Georgia from even running.

Although only a small minority of Democratic leaders are in fact cooperating with the Communists knowingly or unknowingly, they represent a very active influential group and have managed to pull the entire party to the left. This is especially true on policies of national or international scope. Thus for many years, the Democratic Party has done well at the local and State levels but failed in the nationwide contests. It has continued to roll up a majority of seats in Congress and in State legislatures and State governorships, yet has failed to come up with a candidate and a platform that can win Presidential elections.

As previously stated, the American voter will not vote for an openly-admitted Communist. But let the same Communist, while still being a Communist, join the left wing of the Democratic Party, then the Party's regular voters will vote for him as a Democrat, not knowing that they are voting for a Communist or a helper of Communism. This is a shocking state of affairs, which must be corrected so that the voters know whether they are voting for a true Democrat, a Republican, or a Communist or Communist-helper.

Many Democrat voters feel there is something wrong with the Defense and Foreign Policy policies of the Democratic Party, so they vote Republican for President, while voting for Democrats at the State and Local levels.

It is up to true Democrats to require the Communists, "Progressives," and "Forces of Independence" to break away now, rather than wait until later, when they may have seized complete control.

The head of the British Labor Party, Neil Kinnock, once considered a radical, has in fact recently been pushing such a policy of purging his party of many of what the British call "The Loony Left." The Labor Party was facing a situation similar to the Democrats in the U.S.: a long period of losses in national elections to the Conservatives under Margaret Thatcher, who has had the longest run in office of any British Prime Minister in the Twentieth Century.

Kinnock and other Labor leaders decided this was partly the result of voters' suspicions of the Labor Party's left wing, which was pushing such extreme policies as a British withdrawal from NATO, expelling the American bases, and further nationalization of industry, all clearly parallel to the Communist line.

The Democrats in this country are facing the same problems for similar reasons. We must now take equally energetic action to purge our Party of the pro-communist elements.

A prime example is Jesse Jackson and his Rainbow Coalition. Jackson was the second highest vote-getter in the 1988 primaries, billing himself as a "Progressive." Many people would not have voted for him if they had been familiar with his radical record, his association with Jack O'Dell, and his links to Quadaffi, Castro, Ortega, etc.

Yet Jackson almost became the candidate for Vice President. And one of his leading campaign assistants, Ronald Brown, was then made Chairman of the Democratic National Committee. For a time Jackson was promoted as the leading candidate for Mayor of Washington, D.C. to succeed the troubled Mayor Barry. (He later announced he would not run.)

Jackson and his followers had major influence on the Democratic Platform in the 1988 election.

This contained a number of planks paralleling the most radical line, including:

—"ban space weapons in their entirety"

—"mutual moratorium of missile flight testing"

—"halt all nuclear weapons testing"

—"end to support for 'irregular forces' in Central America"

—"declare South Africa a terrorist state" (no mention of the terrorist ANC, which advocates "necklacing," i.e., burning opponents alive."

—"end our counterproductive policy in Angola" (supporting the anti-communist UNITA forces).

—"same day and mail-in voter registration" (which would make it much easier for big city machines, and corrupt groups in general, to register illegal aliens and others susceptible to manipulation).

The result was that Dukakis led the Democrats in a campaign containing many stands paralleling the Communist line, and the Party again went down to one of the worst defeats in history.

Jackson and his Rainbow Coalition should be ousted from the Party. He is not a true Democrat, but is using the Democratic Party as a tool to promote his own radical agenda. A Communist publication, *Political Affairs*, stated this explicitly. In its issue of

March 1989 it said as follows:

> "It seems virtually certain that the Rainbow Coalition and <u>the progressive wing</u> are going to make an all-out effort in 1990 to elect as many progressives or Rainbow-supported candidates as possible in Congressional and state legislative districts won by Jesse Jackson in the 1988 primaries. . .

> "There are bound to be limits on what the (Democratic) party establishment is willing to accommodate, if not tolerate. The struggle over direction will sharpen . . .If it ever comes to a split or a breakaway, the Rainbow Coalition and the progressive wing would be well advised not to leave empty-handed. . .

> "Our (Communist) party can make a unique contribution toward helping the Rainbow achieve its goal of consolidating a mass membership organization corresponding to the size of its electoral support. . .If we show political dexterity, the election of independents—including Communists—could be a component part of this process. . .

> "This much is clear—the overall movement will grow. So will the role of the Rainbow Coalition and the labor movement. And it will unfold in the 1989-1992 quadrennial cycle primarily— but not exclusively—through the <u>medium of the Democratic Party</u>." (e.a.)(2)

Ousting of Jackson should not be considered a racist move. I am not racist, as explained earlier (on pg. 56). There are many fine Black politicians emerging, as Blacks gradually progress up through the ranks following the great strides in civil rights in recent years. Men like David Dinkins, the new Mayor of New York City, and Douglas Wilder, as Governor of Virginia, the first Black State Governor since Reconstruction. These men have attempted to distance themselves from Jackson's radical and anti-Semitic pronouncements.

Such people should be encouraged to move up in the leadership in the Party. We should not continue to tolerate radicals like Jackson and his aides like Jack O'Dell, simply for fear of "losing the Black vote." President Bush won the Presidency almost <u>totally without the Black vote</u>.

In addition, the influence of other radicals who have had close ties with the Communists should be reduced even if there is not enough direct evidence to expel them from the Party completely. These include people like Metzenbaum, Bella Abzug, Dellums, Crockett, Conyers, Edwards, and others who have specific Communist connections or <u>continue to vote paralleling the Communist line.</u>

In such cases we are not talking about guilt by association only, but guilt by both association <u>and action</u>, which is no longer just association. Certainly such people should not be elevated to important committees of Congress and even chairmanships, where they receive classified information.

The Party should take major steps to reduce the influence of the many think tanks and "citizens' organizations" that are influencing the Democratic leadership to move in a pro-communist direction. These include those described more fully in Chapter IV, having many Communists among their personnel,

personnel, or having been identified as Communist fronts before Congressional committees or in State Department publications.

These include the Institute for Policy Studies and its spin-offs such as SANE/Freeze, the Center for National Security Studies, the Center for Defense Information, and the Washington Office on Latin America.

The Party should also take strong steps to reduce the radical influence of such organizations operating within Congress as the Arms Control and Foreign Policy Caucus. As described in Chapter IV this ostensibly non-partisan organization has been taken over almost entirely by the most left-wing elements.

We should encourage only those Democratic leaders who are for a two-party or multi-party system. We should oppose those who are knowingly or unknowingly promoting the aims of one-party advocates, be they Communists or other left-wing or right-wing dictators. Witness the events in China, where the "Peoples' Army" shoots the people. The Army in China is unfortunately an instrument of the State, not the people, or else the Army would not have massacred the brave students who wanted Democracy.

As prior stated, the purpose of this book is to show there are hidden Communists in the Democratic Party. There are also many non-communist Democrats who <u>unknowingly</u> parallel the Communist Party line. Except for the factual material, all other material is the opinion of the author.

To my knowledge, I have not called anyone in this book a Communist who has not admitted that he or she was a Communist or has been so named by a

Congressional Security Committee. If I have failed to do this in specific instances, this is an oversight and these instances should be changed to read "unknown helper(s) of Communism," or "unknowingly helping Communism."

Who are the Communists in the Democratic Party? I have named those who admit they are, I have named many more who have unknowingly paralleled the Communist line in the policies they have supported. Then there are other non-communist Congressmen who unknowingly vote for the Communist line thinking they are loyally voting for the Democratic Party line.

Therefore, I am not naming any other than admitted Communists as "card carrying Communists." I leave that to the experienced Congressional investigators who have the power of Congress behind them. This is the only responsible course to take.

The "knee-jerk" reaction of the Democratic Party is amazing. If the Republican Party is for a bill or a cause, automatically the Democratic Party has to be against it—often without any valid reason except the Republicans were for it. The Communists take advantage of this rivalry between parties for the benefit of Communism.

I have quoted extensively from Communist publications about their policy of infiltrating or using the Democratic Party.

The Communists themselves are the only ones who know fully who are the Communists in the Democrat Party. They will not say who they are, but they do say that they _are_ in the Democratic Party. If I were a Communist, I also would not say who the Communists infiltrated into the Democratic Party were, because then they would be ineffective.

The Democrats deny there are Communists in the Party. Either they do not know or they refuse to acknowledge this problem. But how could they know if the Communists have secretly infiltrated the Party?

It is now up to the Democratic leadership to take active measures about this serious situation. The Democratic Party itself, without anyone demanding they do it, must investigate and then take steps to eliminate such infiltrators together with their non-Communist helpers.

If the Democratic Party refuses to investigate, then it is the duty of Congress to restore the Internal Security Committees and to make the necessary investigations. If Congress refuses to take action, President Bush should empanel a committee of prominent Americans, an equal number of Democrats and Republicans, to investigate this serious condition.

If Congress abdicates this responsibility, all such legislators refusing to take action should be voted out of office for refusing to protect the United States against its domestic enemies.

Congress must restore the functions of the country's internal security organizations. As outlined in the previous chapter, all of this country's official internal security organs have been put out of action: the Senate Internal Security Subcommittee, the House Internal Security Committee, the Subversive Activities Control Board, and the internal security functions of the FBI.

As a result, although the U.S. now spends about 300 billion dollars a year ($300,000,000,000) protecting the Free World against Communism, <u>it does not spend one cent protecting the American people from the actions of American citizens who are coop-</u>

erating with this enemy – Communism – here in the United States.

This is an incredible state of affairs. It is also a dangerous state of affairs because while we are acting on the foreign front, we are ignoring the domestic threat of Communism here in the United States.

This is how the Communists can put over their program here: by funneling all their goals and objectives through the Democratic Party, which is at present the majority party, able to ram through Communist objectives, even over the opposition of the Republicans and many moderate Democrats.

The destruction of our internal security organizations is the best example of how the Communists have been able to work through the Democratic Party to achieve their goals. As described in Chapter V, the Communists stated their objectives clearly in writing 30 years ago to abolish these security organs. The final blows against such organs were made mostly by the Democratic leaders in Congress, such people as Teddy Kennedy, Sam Ervin, Frank Church, and the others as described in Chapter V.

It is time the American people have the same protection against domestic Communism in the United States as the United States spends for its military protection against foreign Communism.

The U.S. Code Title 50 states:

"As a result of evidence adduced before various committees of the Senate and House of Representatives, the Congress finds that:

"1) There exists a world Communist movement which, in its origins, its development, and its current practice, is a world wide revolutionary movement whose purpose it is, by treachery, deceit, infiltration into other groups (governmental and otherwise), espionage, sabotage, terrorism, and any other means deemed necessary, to establish a Communist totalitarian dictatorship in the countries throughout the world through the medium of a world-wide Communist organization.

"2) The establishment of a totalitarian dictatorship in any country results in the suppression of all opposition to the party in power, the subordination of the rights of individuals to the state, the denial of fundamental rights and liberties which are characteristic of a representative form of government, such as freedom of speech, of the press, of assembly, and of religious worship, and result in the maintenance of control over the people through fear, terrorism, and brutality."

In essence, Title 50, Section 781 states that the Communist Party of the USA is not a democratic political party as we know it, but an agent of a foreign government.

Although the Communist Party publicly renounces terrorism, it practices terrorism when it feels necessary, as evidenced by the Communist terrorist forces in El Salvador, who call themselves the FMLN. They are waging a civil war, which is certainly not an act of peace. They talk peace and wage war. We have to pay attention to their actions, not their words. To rely only on their words would lead to disaster and Communist victory.

If they win the struggle in any country, they install the one-party system of Communism. If they lose the struggle, then and only then do they ask to be admitted to a two-party political system and then infiltrate one of the leading parties so that they can still get their Communist platform installed in the political system. While this latter strategy takes longer, the end result can still be Communism.

It is time we restore full protection against this domestic enemy controlled by a foreign power, the Communist Party of the United States.

What can you do personally as a reader of this book?

First, write to your Senator and Congressman that you want a restoration of our domestic subversive protection against these covert agents of a foreign power – the Soviet Union – by reinstating the Senate Internal Security Committee, the House Internal Security Committee, the Subversive Activities Control Board, and the original mandate of the F.B.I.

Second, write your Senators and Congressmen demanding they exclude Communists and their non-communist helpers, including Socialists, from the Democratic and Republican Parties. Communists belong in their own party, the Communist Party, so the voters can know whether they are voting for a true Democrat, Republican, or Communist.

Right now, the American voter does not know whether he or she is voting for a Democrat or a Communist who has joined the Party to use it to further Communist goals – not Democratic goals. This must be changed so the voter knows for whom he or she is voting.

The great Roman orator, Cicero, centuries ago described how traitors can subvert a nation in terms that are descriptive of Communist methods in this century:

> "<u>The Enemy Within.</u> A nation can survive its fools, and even the ambitious. But it cannot survive treason from within. An enemy at the gates is less formidable for he is known and he carries his banners openly. But the traitor moves among those within the gates freely, his sly whispers rustling through all the alleys, heard <u>in the very halls of government itself</u>. For the traitor appears not as a traitor. He wears the common face and their garments, and he appeals to the baseness that lies deep in the hearts of all men. He rots the soul of a nation; he works secretly and unknown in the night to undermine the pillars of a city. <u>He infects the body politic so that it can no longer resist</u>. A murderer is less to be feared." (e.a.)

We must exclude all Communists and "the enemy within," the "progressives" and the "forces of independence" from the Democratic Party. Then and only then will we have true Democrats in the Democratic Party who will vote for the national interest of the United States and not the national interest of the Soviet Union.

If we do nothing, the evils of Communism will prevail. Edmund Burke, the British Member of Parliament and orator (who incidentally supported the cause of the American colonies) once said, "The only thing necessary for the triumph of evil is for <u>good men to do nothing</u>."

All of you who are concerned and want to organize a local chapter of CONCERNED VOTERS to work for the purpose of ejecting the Communists and their helpers from the Democratic Party can contact:

Wilson C. Lucom, Chairman, Concerned Voters, P.O. Box 40309, Washington, D.C. NW 20016.

Ronald V. Dellums - Democratic Socialist

In a recent development, Ed Asner's letter of May 1990 asks for funds for the DEMOCRATIC SOCIALISTS OF AMERICA. Congressman Ron V. Dellums has an insert of a personal letter from his desk. (Exhibit 3) In it Dellums specifically states:

"Changing America takes a politics that is both practical and visionary. I am a member of the Democratic Socialists of America because DSA makes an enormous contribution to building just that kind of movement.

"Make a difference. Join with me and thousands of other Americans who have signed on with the Democratic Socialists of America." (Emphasis added.)

This is exactly what this book is all about. Dellums said, "I am a member of the Democratic Socialists of America." Communists and their non-communist helpers such as Socialists do not belong in the Democratic Party. Ron Dellums must be excluded from the Democratic Party and told to go to the Party of the Democratic Socialists of America, which is definitely not the Democratic Party. It is up to your Congress to take this action.

Remember that the U.S.S.R. stands for Union of Soviet <u>Socialist</u> Republics—a failed system of government.

Dellums is "peddling" the Socialist line in the United States under another name for Socialism—Democratic Socialism. No matter what they call it, it is still Socialism.

Democracy and Socialism are opposed to each other: different systems of government.   Under Socialism our Constitution would be replaced. You cannot be a Democrat and a Socialist at the same time—it is either one or the other. As stated, we have an example of 70 years of Socialism in the Soviet Union that did not work. Why continue with a failing system? We should not, and you should reject Democratic Socialism as a system whose time has passed in failure, which I am sure you do.

Yet as a Socialist, not actually a Democrat, Congressman Dellums introduces Socialist bills, not Democratic bills in Congress, in the name of the Democratic Party. This is outrageous, but both political parties, the Democrats and the Republicans, look the other way because he is black. Black or white makes no difference. What makes a difference, is what party you belong to. Unfortunately, Democratic Party loyalty and "reliability" to the Democratic Party does the rest in getting these Socialist bills passed.

<u>This is precisely how Socialism is being put in place in the United States, through your very own Congress</u>. Socialism can be stopped once it is identified. It all depends on you, the voters, to become active and to write to your elected officials. Otherwise, <u>Socialism will come to the United States</u>. If you do not want Socialism to come to the United States you better become active and oppose it and the Socialist Dellums.

You can really sink your teeth into the Dellums' memo. The evidence is clear that Congressman Dellums is a Democratic <u>Socialist,</u> instead of actually being a Democrat, <u>because he, Ronald V. Dellums, says he is a Democratic Socialist</u>. What more proof do you want? Therefore, he does not belong in the Democratic Party and should be excluded.

Dellums' arrogance in plainly stating he is a Socialist appears to be based on the fact that he believes most American voters just do not care whether or not a man is a Socialist and not a Democrat—even though he is a member of the Democratic Party. The voters also do not understand that you cannot be a Democrat and a Socialist at the same time. The Socialist system calls for <u>state</u> control of everything, the Democratic system calls for the <u>people</u> to control the state and industry.

The vast majority of Democratic Americans are patriotic. I am sure you are; yet you may not believe that what you say or write counts. <u>What you say or write does count</u>. If enough of you write, it counts a whole lot. But, the least you can do is to write. We are not asking you to get a gun and go on the front lines to fight Communism We are asking you to defend the homefront, which is just as important as the military front—in fact more so, in time of no war. But each of you has to do your part.

Show Dellums that you are not indifferent in this case, but do care by writing to your Senators and Congressman asking them to vote to expel Congressman Dellums from the Democratic Party. Ask for a responsive reply because the evidence is positive that Dellums is not a Democrat but a Socialist. If your Representative does not give a responsive reply saying he is going to vote to kick Dellums out of the Democratic Party, tell him you are going to vote against him in the next election because Dellums is an admitted Socialist—no longer a Democrat. This will get his attention.

The time has come for all good Democrats, true liberals, moderates and conservatives, as well as Republicans to demand that the fraudulent Democrats, the Communists, Socialists and helpers of Communism leave the Democratic Party and go to the Communist Party where they really belong. You, personally, can demand that they leave the Democratic Party.

Republicans, this is not just a Democratic issue. It is a Republican issue as well, for if the Socialists take over, there will be no Republican or Democratic Party. More than likely, Jesse Jackson would become President of the United States. Is this what you want?

If you are a Democrat, as I am, you can contact your local Democratic Delegate to the National Democratic Convention and demand he or she propose making the Communists and their helpers quit the Democratic Party and go to the Communist Party.

Until China with over one billion, two hundred million inhabitants, North Korea, Cuba and the many other Communist countries stop being Communist, the United States cannot relax its vigilance against Communism. Remember, the Soviet Union is still turning out one offensive submarine every seven weeks—a machine designed for war. Why would it be doing this if the Soviet Union's real objective was Peace?

Gorbachev talks peace and the Soviet Army prepares for war. Do you believe talk or actions?

Write to, or personally visit, your local newspaper or newspapers. Ask them to write an editorial on Communists and their helpers in the Democratic

Party, citing the Dellum's example and the other examples in this book.

If, at first, they refuse to believe you, show this book to the editor so he will, if he is a fair and honest person, recognize that there are Communists and their helpers in the Democratic Party because the <u>Communists, themselves, say so</u>, as Dellums openly wrote that he was a Socialist. If you can get the media behind this campaign, you will be successful in helping to drive the Communists out of the Democratic Party.

IT ALL DEPENDS ON YOU. WRITE NOW.

NOTES

1. *Washington Post*, 6/22/88, p.A6.
2. p.32.
3. Burnham, "The War We Are In", p. 13.
4. Solzhenitsyn: "Nobel Lecture," p. 24.
5. Cicero, 106-43 B.C.

ACKNOWLEDGEMENTS

I want to express my appreciation for assistance on this book to a very good friend and expert on Communism whose research was invaluable. To Mr. James L. Tyson, President of the Council for the Defense of Freedom, publishers of *The Washington Inquirer*. To Mr. Reed J. Irvine, Chairman of Accuracy in Media Inc. and to Major Sophia Dziadura USAF (Ret.) of Concerned Voters.

EXHIBIT 3

(May 1990)

From the desk of:

Congressman Ronald V. Dellums

Dear Friend,

Our America is a land of many natural resources. But our most important natural resource of all is our people.

As a Congressperson trying to change our national priorities that thought is always on my mind -- whether I'm in Washington or in my own district in California. All too often, and especially so in the past decade, I see the promise and the potential of our people betrayed by the government.

As a senior member of the Armed Services Committee, I have an insider's view as to the senselessness involved in the tens of billions of dollars squandered each year on exotic weapons systems, billions that could end the hunger and hopelessness that grip our nation. In my capacity as Chair of the Congressional Black Caucus, I have helped to lead the fight to reverse the policies that have given tax and program benefits to the rich while the middle class and the poor get lectured on the need to reduce government.

Changing America takes a politics that is both practical and visionary. I am a member of the Democratic Socialists of America because DSA makes an enormous contribution to building just that kind of movement.

Make a difference. Join with me and thousands of other Americans who have signed on with the Democratic Socialists of America.

Sincerely yours,

Ronald V. Dellums

Ronald V. Dellums
Member of Congress

INDEX